Project Railroads You Can Build

from Benchwork to Finished Scenery

Selected by Kent Johnson

KALMBACH
BOOKS

Printed in the United States of America

01 02 03 04 05 06 07 08 09   10 9 8 7 6 5 4 3 2 1

Visit our website at
http://kalmbachbooks.com
Secure online ordering available

Publisher's Cataloging-in-Publication
(Provided by Quality Books, Inc.)

Project railroads you can build / selected by Kent Johnson.
   — 1st ed.
   p. cm.
   ISBN: 0-89024-601-7

   1. Railroads—Models. I. Johnson, Kent J., 1968-

TF197.P76 2001   625.1'9
                           QBI00-940

Art Director: Kristi Ludwig
Graphic Artist: Kelli Colle

The material in this book has previously appeared as articles in *Model Railroader* magazine. They may include an occasional reference to an item elsewhere in the same issue or in a previous issue.

Contents

The Cactus Valley

This 4x8-foot project layout captures the rugged charm of the West

By Dave Frary | Photos by the author

You've probably heard that a layout is really never finished, that the real fun is to spend the rest of your life working on it. I respectfully disagree. I find there's something highly satisfying about building a small model railroad and finishing it! The Cactus Valley is only 4 x 8 feet—just 32 square feet—so there's a good chance you could start and finish it in only a few months.

The plan

The Cactus Valley is suitable for beginning to intermediate modelers. It requires only 16 lengths of code 100 flextrack and one left-hand and three right-hand turnouts. Although it has track on grades, so it wouldn't normally be classed as a beginner's layout, I don't think that should hold anyone back.

In keeping with the idea of a beginner's layout, my first purchase was two train sets: Life-Like's Union Pacific Diesel Master set and Mantua's El Grande Express. I replaced the horn hook couplers with Kadee and Life-Like knuckle couplers and substituted Life-Like Proto 2000 metal wheels on the freight cars. As the layout doesn't make use of anything except the

Dave Frary's HO scale Cactus Valley captures the rugged scenery of the West in just 4 x 8 feet. Due to his spray can foam scenery techniques the layout is lightweight.

rolling stock, you could just as easily purchase cars and locomotives that match your preferences. The curves and clearances are okay as long as you stay with 40- or 50-foot cars and eight-wheel diesels. If you like steam, 2-6-0s and 2-8-0s would be appropriate for this layout.

The Cactus Valley is a mythical place, but it's a place that could have been. For modeling resources, I used John Sayer's The Santa Fe, Prescott & Phoenix Railway (Pruett Publishing Co.) and John Olson's Jerome & Southwestern project layout which ran in *Model Railroader* from 1982 to '83 and was republished by Kalmbach Books as *Building an HO Model Railroad with Personality* (out of print). John also loaned me photos he and his wife, Katie, took while on vacation in Arizona; my thanks to them both.

Modeling the model

Before I start a layout I like to see the plan in three dimensions, so I

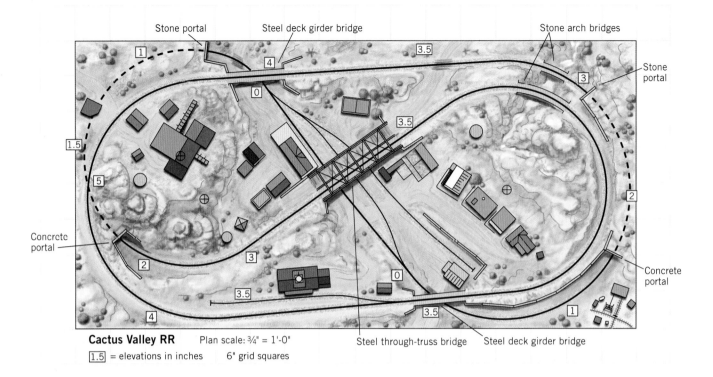

Stone portal · Steel deck girder bridge · Stone arch bridges · Stone portal

Concrete portal

Concrete portal

Steel through-truss bridge · Steel deck girder bridge

Cactus Valley RR   Plan scale: ¾" = 1'-0"

1.5 = elevations in inches   6" grid squares

build a small clay model first. I made several copies of my track plan and glued them to thin shirt cardboard. I cut out around the track and placed these pieces on a heavy cardboard base, then used little bits of cardboard to elevate the tracks.

I formed the scenery with modeling clay. As I added clay, I studied the terrain looking for scenic possibilities. On a layout this size you get visual impact by using scenic features as screens to isolate each area of the layout from the others. Doing this kind of model doesn't stop you from making changes later, but it means you'll have a better sense of what you can realistically achieve.

Building two frames

The benchwork is in two parts: a 4 x 8-foot frame made of 1 x 3 pine, with all joints glued and screwed, sits on a smaller frame with legs. I added casters to the leg frame so that I could easily rotate the layout for pictures; they'd also be handy for rolling the layout into a corner when not in use.

Why two frames? For starters, it makes the layout twice as sturdy.

Second, the layout can be lifted off the bottom frame for transport or storage.

The lower frame can be disassembled into a top and two leg units. I screwed my legs and braces to their frame top, as I expect to transport it only occasionally. If you're going to disassemble it a lot, then bolts and wing nuts would be a better choice.

Laying out the track plan

Lay a piece of ⅜" plywood on the frame and draw the track plan full size in pencil. Next, using a strip of cork roadbed mark lines on either side of the track center line. As the cutting diagram shows, you need to redraw and cut the ground-level piece on the left side from a different part of the plywood since you have a track crossing above it. I cut the trackbed from the plywood with a saber saw, allowing an extra ½" on either side of the lines. I didn't cut away the trackbed at the bridges until after all the track was in and running.

Before adding risers, I set a level on the layout frame and shimmed between it and the leg frame with strips of cardboard, leveling it both

Upper right: Shots like this make you forget all about the fact that this is a small layout. The bridge in the background accommodates both railroad and vehicular traffic, though lots of drivers don't care for the sensation and will wait until the train is gone before crossing.

north and south and east and west. If you aren't using casters, you can purchase leveling bolts at hardware stores that install into the legs and use them to level the layout.

For the risers I used 1 x 2 and 1 x 3 pine. I clamped each riser in place under the trackbed, wiggled it up or down until the height was correct, leveled it, then tightened the clamp. Then I checked everything again, drilled the pilot holes, and added the screws. I also put the plywood shelf that serves as the base for the mine on 1 x 3 risers.

Laying roadbed and track

I use cork roadbed because I like its sound-deadening properties and ease of use. I run a bead of white glue down each side of the center line, then lay a cork strip on each side and staple it to hold it in place until the glue dries.

6

Tools needed for this project:

Cordless drill
Pilot drill with countersink
1", 1½", and 2" drywall screws
Framing square
Tape measure
Circular saw
Saber saw
Radius templates made from styrene
Upholstery hammer
Nail set
Sanding block
Motor tool with a heavy-duty cutoff disk
Stanley Surform tool
Levels
Soldering iron, solder, and flux
Liquid Nails for projects
1" Styrofoam beadboard
Great Stuff foam sealan

The upper frame will hold the layout itself and can be removed for storage or transportation. The compact leg unit can also be disassembled or simply stowed in a corner.

At turnouts, I run one piece of cork right through on the straight side of the turnout and then run the other piece out the diverging route. I then fill in the center using a single-edge razor blade to cut the cork to fit.

The next day I remove the staples from the roadbed with pliers and smooth any irregularities in the cork with a sanding block.

I prepare my flextrack by soldering the sections into pairs. I remove a couple of ties from both ends of each length, add rail joiners, and solder them together.

This helps the curves stay in gauge and free of kinks. I start by centering a couple sections on a curve and working out to the straight track.

Using the center line of the cork roadbed as my guide, I pin the track in place as I go by driving in track nails just enough to hold. Where rail has to be cut I use rail nippers, then smooth the end with a heavy-duty cutoff wheel in my Dremel motor tool.

When all the track is in place, I sink the track nails to the tops of the ties with a small hammer and a nail set (don't go too far or the ties will bend and narrow the gauge). Then I test-run the trains.

On both big curves I found the track tipped out. To cure this, I shimmed the outside rail by slipping squares of shirt cardboard under the tie strip. I raised the rail by eye and repeatedly ran the trains back and forth until it looked right. Then I removed each cardboard shim, ran it through a bead of white glue, and pushed it back in place.

Wiring

Because the Cactus Valley is just a simple folded loop with one siding and a spur, the wiring is simple. I drilled holes on either side of the track and soldered feeders to the rails at the locations shown on the track plan. I stapled the feeder wires to the tops of the 1 x 3 pine frame and routed them to a terminal strip under the layout.

This layout would be perfectly well served by any stock power pack. However I wanted to try DCC technology, so I selected an MRC 2000 DCC system to control the trains and powered it with one of the train set transformers.

Finishing the track

After several days of running trains to be sure the layout ran properly, I covered the switch points with bits of masking tape, then sprayed the track with Floquil Rail Brown. Before the paint cured, I cleaned the rail tops with a rag soaked with Floquil's Dio-Sol thinner.

The next day I lightly drybrushed the ties with Polly Scale Reefer White to make them look sun-bleached. To drybrush, simply dip your brush in paint and wipe off all the paint. A small residue will remain on the bristles and produce

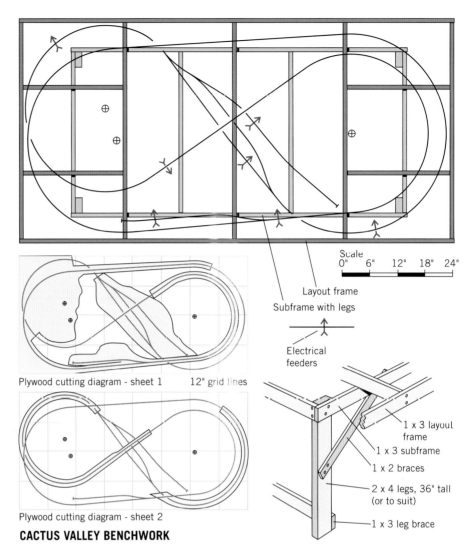

Plywood cutting diagram - sheet 1   12" grid lines

Plywood cutting diagram - sheet 2

CACTUS VALLEY BENCHWORK

Scale
0"   6"   12"   18"   24"

Layout frame
Subframe with legs

Electrical feeders

1 x 3 layout frame
1 x 3 subframe
1 x 2 braces
2 x 4 legs, 36" tall (or to suit)
1 x 3 leg brace

a very light coat on the object being painted.

The turnouts are all within easy reach, so I used Caboose Industries ground throws to operate them. I shortened the switch rods and drilled a hole in each to accept the ground throw's pin. Then I glued the ground throws to squares of .060" styrene which I then glued to the trackbed.

Scenery profile boards

The profile boards are ⅛" untempered Masonite hardboard. They dress up the sides of the layout and support the edge of the scenery.

Using my clay model as a guide, I used a saber saw to cut them to the approximate profile. Then I temporarily screwed them to the sides

and ends of the layout and after much contemplation recut the profile in several places. I then permanently attached the boards using Liquid Nails. Slight mismatches at the corners were filled with spackling compound and sanded smooth.

Building the tunnels

I now turned to building tunnels. For this and much of the rest of my scenery I used beadboard—that's the white, crumbly Styrofoam. I purchased mine in 24" x 36" sheets at a craft store.

I started by cutting a bunch of strips of 1" beadboard roughly 2½" x 7" and gluing them to the underside of the trackbed with 2" protruding from either side. The adhesive I used was Liquid Nails for

It's always interesting when tracks cross over one another, and the bridge provides a handy place to add a sign giving the railroad some identity. A little weathering makes that Mantua GP20 look like a veteran desert rat.

Projects, which won't dissolve Styrofoam. These strips support the tunnel base and walls, which are also made of 1″ beadboard.

The wall bases were cut to fit the contour of the trackbed and glued on top of the supports. On top of them I glued the interior walls. I wanted the walls to curve at the same radius as the trackbed, so I scribed them about halfway through every 2″ on the outer side using a serrated knife. This allowed the beadboard to be gently flexed to the curve of the track and glued in place.

I added walls only where they could be seen. The rest of the tunnels were left open so I could reach the track from below in case of a derailment. I painted the interior a dark gray made from equal parts of my base earth color (Sears Easy Living 589 Sage-BC) and a flat black interior paint.

Along each side of the tunnel tracks I simulated rock rubble by mixing coarse Paint 'n Tex with the dark gray paint and applying it with a stiff brush. (Paint 'n Tex is a crushed-foam texturing additive.) Finally, I ballasted the tunnel track using a pinkish decomposed granite from Arizona Rock & Mineral Company, no. 1093. I poured the ballast between the rails and spread it with a soft brush, making sure to keep the ballast off the tops of the ties.

When all the ballast was in place, I wet it with wet water (water with a drop or two of dishwashing detergent added to lower its viscosity) and dripped on diluted acrylic matte medium (4 parts water to 1 part matte medium). The next day I darkened the ballast slightly with a black wash. I ballasted the layout in small sections as I finished the surrounding scenery.

The Woodland Scenics tunnel portals were painted on the workbench, then glued at each end of the tunnel. It's important to use a National Model Railroad Association clearance gauge when placing the portals so the track is centered in the opening.

Finally, I glued a black beadboard roof on top of the tunnel walls to keep out debris.

Bridges and abutments

I assembled and painted the steel bridges at the workbench. To install them, I removed a section of track slightly longer than the bridge, then set the bridge on the cork. After marking its length on the roadbed and adding the thickness of the abutments at each end of the bridge, I cut away the trackbed with a saber saw.

I glued the abutments to the ends of the trackbed, making sure they were level with the top of the cork roadbed, clamped them in place, and let them dry overnight.

Then I applied a thick coat of acrylic gesso (used by artists to prepare canvas) to the abutments to seal the wood and give it texture. You could substitute thick white acrylic paint. When dry, I painted the abutments with a mixture of equal parts Polly Scale Foundation, Earth, and White.

I used expanding foam to merge the abutment into the scenery. I've been experimenting with these spray-on, polyurethane foams for several years and have developed a set of easy-to-use techniques. In the next chapter I'll describe how I use Great Stuff, a foam sealant made to fill cracks and holes around the house, for my basic scenery shell. This spray-on expanding foam makes a lightweight, almost indestructible shell that will withstand bumps and flexing.

Bill of materials

White glue
8-foot pine 1 x 3 (12)
8-foot pine 1 x 2 (1)
8-foot 2 x 4 (2)
4 x 8⅜" plywood (1 1/2)
4 x 8 Masonite (3)
Paint 'n Tex

Arizona Rock & Mineral
1093 ballast

Atlas
168 code 100 flextrack (16)
860 left-hand turnout
861 right-hand turnout (3)
2540 track nails
170 rail joiners (2)

Caboose Industries
218 manual ground throws (4)

Central Valley
1903 single-track girder bridge (2)

Evergreen
9060 .060" styrene sheet

Feather Lite
4204 portal wings (4)
43000 abutment (4)

Floquil/Polly S
130007 Rail Brown spray paint

Kadee
no. 28 couplers (5)

Kibri
9652 bridge

Life-Like
21096 Proto 2000 couplers (5)
21257 Proto 2000 36" wheelsets (4)

Micro Mark
80437 Bright Bar track cleaning pad

Midwest Industries
3015 five-pack HO cork roadbed (4)

Once the track boards are in place, Dave adds the cork roadbed. He staples the cork to hold it in place until the glue dries, then removes the staples and smooths the cork with a sanding block.

The track is held in place with track nails pushed into the cork. After it's all in and double-checked, Dave sets the nails flush with the tie tops using a hammer and nail set.

To correct the outward cant of the plywood on the big curves, Dave shimmed the track with shirt cardboard. The Styrofoam blocks glued underneath will support the tunnel walls.

Model Rectifier Corporation
MRC 2000 DCC control system
AD300 decoder
AD310 decoder

Polly Scale paint
414113 Reefer White
414131 Aged White
414311 Earth

Walthers
933-3012 double-track bridge
904-470 Solvaset

Woodland Scenics
C1252 concrete portal
C1253 cut stone portal
C1255 random stone portal

X-acto
7003 small clamps
7004 large clamps

Wiring the Cactus Valley is simplicity itself. Feeder wires like those shown here are soldered to the rail at the points indicated on the track plan.

Drybrushing with white paint gives the ties a sun-bleached effect typical of desert railroads.

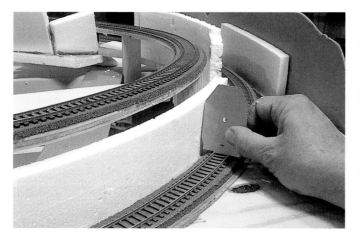

Dave checks clearances with an NMRA HO standards gauge. He scribed the beadboard every few inches so it would curve easily.

Tunnel portals were checked with a level and held in place until the glue dried. One of the hardboard scenery profile boards appears in the background.

After testing the track thoroughly, Dave removed the sections at the bridges and cut away the roadbed. Then he installed the abutments, glued the bridges in, and re-laid the track across the tops. Some of the abutments are wood painted with acrylic gesso.

The tunnel walls extend only as far as you can see through the portal. Dave painted and weathered the bridges before installing them. The girder bridges use commercial abutments.

Scenery for the Cactus Valley

Foam shell scenery is lightweight and easy to use

By Dave Frary | Photos by the author

Now that we've built the benchwork, laid the track, wired it, and test-run some trains, we'll begin by spraying, carving, and coloring our foam scenery base. Once the ground cover is in place, we'll add one of those small towns that still echoes with the sounds and look of the Old West.

Foam scenery shell

For my scenic base I used Great Stuff, a "minimal expanding foam sealant." It's made to fill cracks and holes around the house, sets tack-free in 15 minutes, and cures completely in eight hours. Great Stuff sticks to nearly everything, so wear latex gloves, old clothes, and eye protection while you apply it. Most importantly, wear an organic filter respirator to keep the fumes out of

Dave Frary's HO scale Cactus Valley is set in the modern West, but the Old West has left its traces on Main Street, and the scenery is timeless.

Cut, fit, and glue sheets of 1"-thick beadboard to cover all flat areas. Then spray Great Stuff foam over it. Don't forget to cover the track with masking tape. Frame the areas surrounding the arched bridges with beadboard, then spray foam to fill the gaps and to provide contours. Apply the foam starting at the bottom and work upward. The resulting shell is about 2" thick. After it sets, shape with a serrated knife, which usually removes ¾" to 1" of foam.

The foam is easily controlled. Even so, cover anything you don't want it to stick to. Use wads of paper to make the land forms, holding it in shape with masking tape.

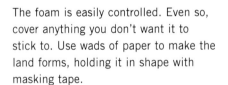

Next cover all the paper with plastic food wrap. After the foam has set, pull out the paper and plastic from below the layout.

Cut away any foam that oozed onto profile boards, portals, or track, and remove the masking tape. Dave cut around the hills over the hidden track and lifted them off for shaping at the workbench. Later, he glued them back with a bead of Great Stuff foam.

Dave used a serrated knife to carve and trim the foam in most places, but a Stanley Surform tool came in handy for flattening large areas and providing a rougher texture.

your lungs. Read the instructions on the can and observe all the safety precautions.

I spread a plastic dropcloth under the layout to catch drips and covered anything I didn't want it to stick to with masking tape. After spraying the foam, don't touch it! Open the windows, turn on a fan, and go away until tomorrow. This foam needs air to cure completely and it emits relatively harmless gases while curing.

If you spray foam where you don't want it, make sure it's fully set, then remove it by chipping away with a small screwdriver. On track, any remaining bits of foam can be removed with a copper-bristled suede brush.

Rocks and retaining walls

All the retaining walls, like those in the photo on page 12, were made from beadboard (the familiar white Styrofoam). I troweled a thin coat of ScaleCrete over the surface to seal it and give it a concrete look. After the ScaleCrete dried I painted it with Polly Scale Concrete. I cast my rocks using Mountains in Minutes two-part Polyfoam in rubber molds. Foam rocks are lightweight and easy to color so they look just like the real thing. I chose molds that had well-defined strata, like the rocks I'd seen in photos of the desert.

I set the molds in a box of packing peanuts and pushed the peanuts around until the molds were level and fully supported. Then I sprayed them with Scotchgard Fabric Protector which keeps the foam from sticking to the mold and ruining it.

I mixed the Polyfoam in a 10-ounce paper cup and drizzled just enough into each mold to barely cover the bottom. To force the foam into all the nooks and crannies, I cover each mold with plastic food wrap and over this place a board with a brick on top. In about 20 minutes, when the mold is cool to the touch, I carefully peel it away from the foam casting. I saw off the back of most castings so they're less than 1″ thick. This way they're flexible and easy to shape to the scenery base.

On a whim, I grabbed a handful of foam shavings, bunched them up, wrapped them with masking tape, and plunked the result on a hill. The result reminded me of the monument rocks in Arizona, so I made several more.

Paint and texture

For the base color of my desert I bought a gallon of Sears Easy Living 589 Sage-BC. I also bought a quart of a slightly lighter earth color, Sears Easy Living 059 Golden Muffin-ABC. Other paint stores can mix identical colors. I also purchased a quart each of flat black and flat white interior latex, and a tube each of Medium Yellow and Red Oxide Tinting Colors. On a whim I purchased a spray can of American Accents Stone Creations. This is speckle paint—it sprays minute drops of black, white, and a beige earth color—used to duplicate the color and texture of stone. It's an easy way to add a heavy gravel texture to the scenery, and the more I used it, the more I liked it.

In a pump sprayer bottle I mixed 16 ounces of black wash. I started with three tablespoons (or more) of India ink, added several drops of Joy dishwashing detergent, and filled the bottle with water. I then filled another 16-ounce spray bottle with wet water, which I would use to mix and blend colors on the layout. For mixing tinting colors I collected a bunch of eight-ounce yogurt containers with resealable lids. I used an assortment of Arizona Rock and Minerals ballast, rock powders, and gravel for ground texture. I also used several coffee cans full of finely sifted sand. Sand is available at building supply stores and adds a real sparkle to the scenery.

Spray the rock castings with black from one direction and with an earth color from the opposite side. Break castings into smaller pieces to fill gaps.

These rocks were glued with Liquid Nails for Projects, and left to dry overnight.

Dave used two techniques to blend the castings into the scenery. In areas needing little fill, he used drywall joint compound. The rocks behind the bridges were embedded in a Gypsolite base (use Sculptamold as a substitute). Push the rock castings in place, then smooth the Gypsolite with a wet brush.

Indian Head rock and most of the other monument rocks were made by standing foam scraps in a swirl of foam then doing some final carving. Balancing Rock was the top of a mountain sliced off, turned upside down, and stuck back in place on a toothpick.

To seal the foam, put a glop of joint compound into a small bucket and mix in several handfuls of the Paint 'n Tex and thin with water to reach a honey-like consistency. Then brush it on using horizontal strokes to create strata.

Paint bands of red and yellow across the mountains to give the effect of strata.

Spray wet water to blend the bright colors. Use the Sage to highlight rock faces.

Lightly spray some speckle paint around the rocks, on vertical surfaces, and on the tops of hills. Let dry undisturbed for a few hours.

Brush a 1:2 mix of white glue and water on all the flat areas of the layout, then sprinkle on the sand. Add texture with a mix of Paint 'n Tex, joint compound, and Sage paint.

Use Sedona Red rock powder to represent red earth and mine tailings. If it's too strong, use a wet brush to spread the pigment over the scenery. Seal it by spraying with a cheap, extra-hold hair spray. While it's wet, you can sprinkle on grass, twigs, and small stones.

Paint everything, except the track and rock castings, with the basic earth color (Sage) mixed 1:1 with water. Over this lightly dust Scenic Express Scrub Grass Blend, then paint in dark shadows under the rock overhangs using the black wash.

Vegetation and water

Though deserts may be arid, they're hardly devoid of life. Water and plant life are just as important to a desert layout as they are to one set in the forested Northeast. In fact it may be even more important, because you can't just cover the hills with forest. I wanted to capture the general look of the desert, but without building each individual plant.

Cactus Valley vegetation consists of shapes and textures gleaned from my stack of prototype photos. I started by making the low vegetation with white poly fiberfill (pillow stuffing from the fabric store) and Woodland Scenics Green Poly Fiber FP-178. The white poly fiber was stretched into thin sheets and spray-painted with gray, brown, and black flat auto primers. In some places where I wanted to tint the desert only lightly with low, grass-like growth, I saturated the ground with hair spray and sprinkled on traces of scenic foam. Around the structures and in the mine area I mixed pencil-sharpener shavings and small pieces of sphagnum moss with the Scrub Grass Blend for different texture. This, plus a few strategically placed cactus plants and pine trees, completed the sparse vegetation.

In the desert, if there's a town, there's water, so the small stream is fully justified. I poured the stream using Enviro-Tex Lite, which is a two-part epoxy used for counter and table tops.

Structures

I built the roads after I had worked out locations for the buildings. This was especially important on the sloping main street. I chose easy-to-build plastic and wood kits that had a Western flavor. They're all built following their directions, except I modified the Walthers stockyard to fit a smaller area by the tracks. I primed, painted, and lightly weathered them with washes of artist's oil paints. I drybrushed each with Polly Scale White to bring out the detail.

The main street of Cactus Valley runs uphill. I used a single piece of beadboard as the base for this whole area. The photos show how I made the foundations for the buildings along here. Structures like the depot and businesses on the cross street at the bottom of the hill rest on flat ground. These I simply glued down with a bead of white glue. I always use weights to hold buildings level until the glue dries.

The two Grandt Line mines were each built at the workbench on a sheet of foam, painted, and completely detailed prior to installation. Their foam bases were blended into the surrounding scenery using Sculptamold. Several of the smaller structures were made by Model Die Casting in the 1970s and are no longer manufactured. If you look around you can find some small adobe-like structures that can substitute for these.

Finishing the layout

To give the layout a lived-in look I placed hundreds of small details around the structures and along the

To represent low scrub growth, pull off small pieces of the brown and green poly-fill and stretch them into thin, almost invisible, wafers. Lay the poly fiber on the scenery, pulling out the edges as thin as possible. Soak with cheap hair spray and sprinkle on Flock & Turf ground cover. Use more hair spray if needed.

Prepare the Scenic Express 6"-high lodge-pole pines for planting by spraying their undersides with brown and the tops of the branches dark green. To finish, spray a mist of light green over the tips of the branches.

Seal the streambed with acrylic gloss medium, brushing it around the rocks and the lower edges of the bridges. At the base of the small waterfall glue a piece of clear styrene to the rocks with gloss medium and let it dry for several days. Then, starting at the top, pour a little Enviro-Tex Lite into the bed and push it down the mountain and over the waterfall using a disposable brush. Unwind the fuzz from the end of a Q-Tip, soak it in Enviro-Tex, and drape it over the falls to look like foam-filled water. Now continue working the Enviro-Tex downstream. As described in the Enviro-Tex instructions, use a heat gun to remove trapped bubbles.

The cacti are resin and plastic castings from Plastruct and MLR. Spray them with green paint and sprinkle Noch Green Flocking into the wet paint to represent the needles. That's Balancing Rock in the back.

Pieces of Woodland Scenics Green Poly Fiber were pulled and shaped into small balls to make sagebrush. Most of these were glued on the layout, then sprinkled with foam. Some were left bare to represent tumbleweeds.

A wrecked car, the town water tank, and even some blooms on the cactus turn this minor corner of the layout into an interesting scene.

TOP LEFT: Make the base of the road and structures from 1″ beadboard. Set each building in place and cut around it with a sharp knife, then push up the downhill end until it's level. Squirt a bead of white glue around the edges to hold it in place.

TOP RIGHT: Paint the bases to look like concrete or stone and the land earth color.

The Walthers Sunrise Feed Mill became Flying Rock Mining Supply. Little details like a scale, sacks, barrel, and LPG tank really bring a scene to life.

Glue down the .040″ sheet styrene roads with Liquid Nails. Trowel Sculptamold along the edges to blend them into the surrounding area. As the Sculpatamold starts to set, scrape the road (and track) clean and smooth. Paint the road and shoulders with undiluted Sage paint.

track. I call these "cheap details"— little scraps that give the layout a lived-in look.

I save bits of painted wood left over from kit construction, old fences, phone poles, barrels, corrugated siding, plant twigs, branches with bark texture, and painted parts from wood and metal kits. Some of these scraps are dunked in the black wash or drybrushed with white to age them. I glue them in small piles and clusters using white glue. It's this kind of clutter that can change a layout from looking nicely detailed to looking real.

I brushed black wash over people and animal figures, letting it settle and dry in the crevices. After the wash dried, I lightly drybrushed each figure with diluted Polly Scale Reefer White. Some of the figures were on stands which I surgically removed with a hobby knife.

Sprinkle fine sand into the wet paint through a tea strainer. Add just enough sand so that all the moisture in the paint is absorbed. After it dries, vacuum up any loose sand. Now is a good time to go back and clean all the rail on the layout.

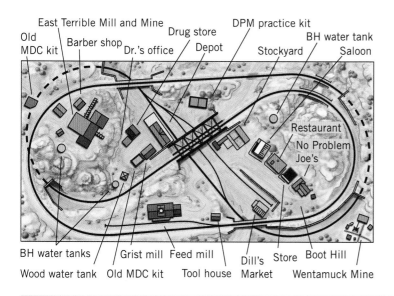

East Terrible Mill and Mine
Old MDC kit
Barber shop
Dr.'s office
Drug store
DPM practice kit
Depot
Stockyard
BH water tank
Saloon

Restaurant
No Problem Joe's

BH water tanks
Grist mill
Feed mill
Wood water tank
Old MDC kit
Tool house
Dill's Market
Store
Boot Hill
Wentamuck Mine

Grandt Line East Terrible Mill & Mining was built at the workbench, then installed on the layout.

Bill of materials

American Accents
Stone Creations speckle paint

American Art Clay Co.
Sculptamold (5 pounds)

American Model Builders
122 Dill's Market
135 mercantile
138 depot

Arizona Rock & Mineral Co.
107-03 high desert ground
1040 Sedona red
1172 mauve ballast
1175 desert mauve chips
1232 reddish tan ballast
1310 mill tailings
1410 sunset orange
1420 Supai red

BH Models
310 water tank (3)

Campbell
374 grist mill
366 drug and barber shop

Design Preservation
Models
360 learning kit

Environmental Technology
Enviro-Tex Lite

Evergreen styrene
.040" styrene sheet

Grandt Line
5900 saloon
5901 East Terrible mill
5902 Wentamuck mine
5905 tool house
5906 No Problem Joe's

IHC
810 Luigi's restaurant

Life-Like
1125 railroad signs

Main Street Graphics
1123 curtains

MLR
5301 saguaro cactus

Mountains in Minutes
Polyfoam

Paint 'n Tex
fine
coarse

Plastruct
94071 prickly pear cactus

Rix
30 telephone poles

ScaleCrete
32-ounce ScaleCrete

Sears Easy Living paint
589 Sage-BC, gallon
059 Golden Muffin-ABC, quart
red tint
yellow tint

Walthers
3047 stockyard
3061 feed mill

Woodland Scenics
178 poly fiber (green)
224 Doctor's office

Miscellaneous
organic filter respirator
drywall joint compound
paintbrushes
spray paint
    black automotive primer
    brown automotive primer
    earth tone
    light green
    medium green
    dark green

The Northwest Timber Co.

HO SCALE

This project layout goes a step beyond the traditional 4 x 8 layout

By Lionel Strang | Photos by the author

When Jim Kelly, *Model Railroader's* managing editor, asked me if I'd like to build a beginner's layout, I thought it would be the ideal project to show what a great family hobby model railroading can be.

Although neither Anne nor Peter, my wife and son, are model railroaders, Anne has always supported my hobby and lent her artistic eye to my work, and Peter is always keen to build things. Both were happy to lend a hand in this project and excited by the results.

I figured it would be relatively easy to build a small beginner's layout, after all my own HO scale Allegheny & Lackawanna Southern occupies a 20 x 30-foot room. What I discovered was that building a small layout was as rewarding and as challenging as a large one.

Design

Any layout I build must have plenty of interesting scenery and structures for good photo opportunities, and it must be fun to operate. I worked

Lionel Strang built the Northwest Timber Co. as a family project with his wife, Anne, and son, Peter. The HO scale layout is six feet square, but its top is a standard 4 x 8-foot sheet of plywood.

out the concept for the layout with George Sebastian-Coleman at MR, who then came up with the track plan.

To meet my goals of interesting scenery and structures, yet keep it simple to build, we designed the layout around the Walthers Trees and Trains series and set it in the Pacific Northwest. During construction I made a few changes.

The plan creates two independent scenes, a sawmill and a paper mill, on opposite sides of the backdrop. Beyond the short leg of the L-shaped backdrop are two staging tracks that provide for interesting operations.

The Northwest Timber Co. at work

Operations on the NTC consist of three basic trains. An NTC log train enters through the tunnel from staging. It brings in timber loads to the sawmill or pulp loads to the paper mill and returns to the woods with empty log cars and pulp racks.

The same engine can now return and work the sawmill to paper mill turn, delivering sawdust and pulpwood culled from the sawmill to the rotary dumper at the paper mill and setting out loaded paper cars and finished lumber on the interchange track.

The Union Pacific train comes out of staging from the other direction to the paper mill where it delivers chemicals in tank cars and covered hoppers. It then picks up the loads on the interchange track and drops off empty lumber racks and boxcars for paper, which the NTC turn will spot. You can either see the sawmill as the end of the UP turn and make getting the engine back on the other end of the train part of the fun, or you can run the train on around the layout as if this is one stop on a longer run.

Powering up

To keep the layout fun to operate I decided to use to use MRC's Command Control 2000, an entry-level DCC system (Digital Command Control). For more on DCC, see *Basic Model Railroading*, available from Kalmbach Books.

Using DCC does require decoders in your locomotives. For the NTC I chose Life-Like's SD9 which comes with a decoder plug already installed. All I had to was pop off the shell, plug in the decoder, and close it up again. I painted this engine and numbered it 198 for the Northwest Timber Co. The SD9 was designed for heavy work on light rail, exactly the situation on logging lines.

For the Union Pacific engine, I purchased a Kato GP35 and had a Digitrax decoder installed by my good friend, Norm Stenzel. Since then, System One has released drop-in replacements for the Kato circuit boards with a decoder built in.

If you wanted to model an earlier era, you could use a Rivarossi Heisler or a Roundhouse/Model Die Casting Shay, both geared steam engines, for the NTC, and an SD9 or Bachmann's new 2-8-0 for the UP engine.

Well, that's what we wanted to build. Now we'll show you how we did it in photos and captions.

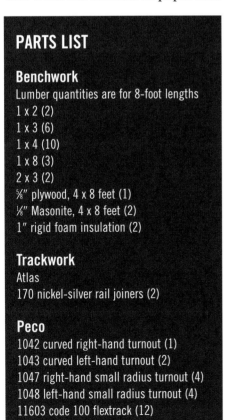

PARTS LIST

Benchwork
Lumber quantities are for 8-foot lengths
1 x 2 (2)
1 x 3 (6)
1 x 4 (10)
1 x 8 (3)
2 x 3 (2)
⅝" plywood, 4 x 8 feet (1)
⅛" Masonite, 4 x 8 feet (2)
1" rigid foam insulation (2)

Trackwork
Atlas
170 nickel-silver rail joiners (2)

Peco
1042 curved right-hand turnout (1)
1043 curved left-hand turnout (2)
1047 right-hand small radius turnout (4)
1048 left-hand small radius turnout (4)
11603 code 100 flextrack (12)

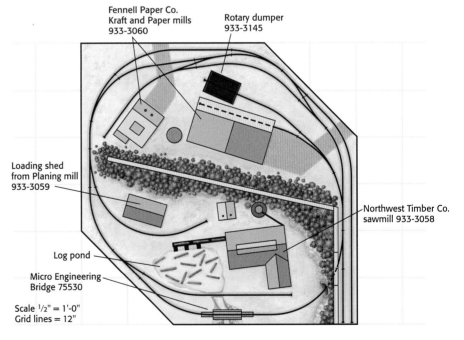

Fennell Paper Co.
Kraft and Paper mills
933-3060

Rotary dumper
933-3145

Loading shed
from Planing mill
933-3059

Northwest Timber Co.
sawmill 933-3058

Log pond

Micro Engineering
Bridge 75530

Scale ½" = 1'-0"
Grid lines = 12"

Follow the drawings below and cut four 2 x 3 legs and screw each pair to the 1 x 3 cross braces. At the top, place a 1 x 4 joist. This gives a final track height of about 42″; you can make it shorter or taller to suit you.

The L girders are just pieces of 1 x 4 glued and screwed at right angles to each other. Build two, turn the legs upside down, position them 18″ from the end of the L girders, and screw (don't glue) the pieces together.

Once the legs are attached, turn the frame right-side up and screw 1 x 3 longitudinal braces to the inside of the L girder. The bracing should run from the center of the girder down to a foot above the floor.

Attach the bracing to the legs with a gusset made from ⅜″ plywood. Building the frame is one place a family can really work together. Anne and Peter were invaluable helping to hold and screw parts in place.

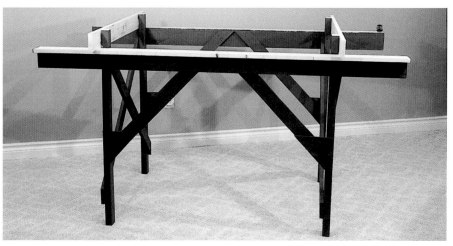

Once this part of the benchwork was completed, I painted the legs and any areas that would be seen under the layout dark forest green. The fascia that was added later was also painted dark green. In the end, this gives the whole layout a nice finished look.

LEG DETAILS
SCALE ½″ = 1'-0"

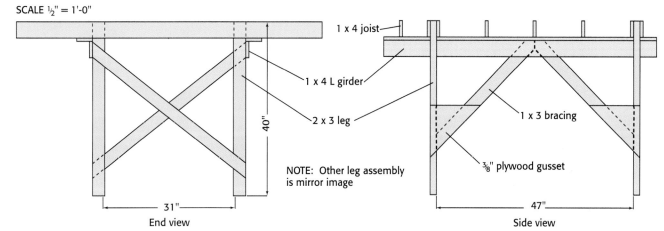

31″

40″

End view

1 x 4 joist

1 x 4 L girder

2 x 3 leg

NOTE: Other leg assembly is mirror image

1 x 3 bracing

⅜″ plywood gusset

47″

Side view

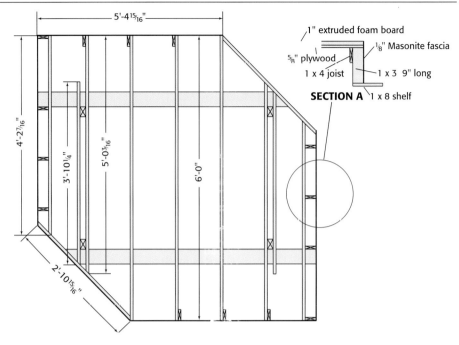

George's six-sided design had me scratching my head until I realized that I was approaching the problem from the wrong angle. Rather than treat the layout as six-sided, I simply treated it as a six-foot square with two corners cut off and came up with the frame shown here. For more information on benchwork see *How to build Model Railroad Benchwork,* by Linn Westcott, published by Kalmbach.

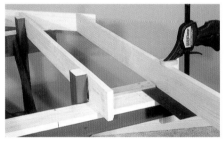

Next add the three six-foot joists between the legs. Screw these on from below as Peter is doing, so that you can easily move them if you need to. Close spacing of joists means that ⅝" plywood will be sufficient to form a rigid tabletop.

Cut the plywood as shown on page 26 and arrange atop the joists. Place a piece of 1 x 4 at the two corners over the exposed L girder and mark where to trim. Remove the plywood and the two short joists to trim where you marked.

Replace the short joists and add the angled ones. For the outer ones, I found it easiest to cut the 45-degree angle on one end, butt it up to the angled joist, and trim the other end to length.

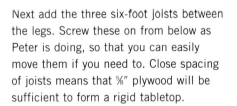

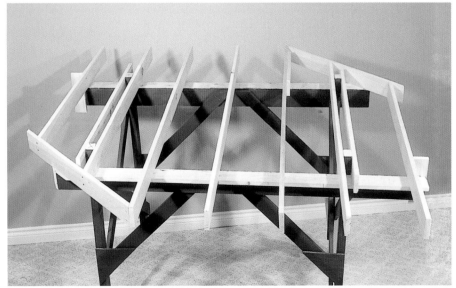

Attach 9"-long pieces of 1 x 3 to the ends of each joist and across the ends. These will support the fascia (the trim board around the layout) and by screwing a 1 x 6 across their bottom ends you have a handy shelf. The completed benchwork requires only to have the plywood pieces screwed in place.

PLYWOOD CUTTING PLAN
SCALE ½" = 1'-0"

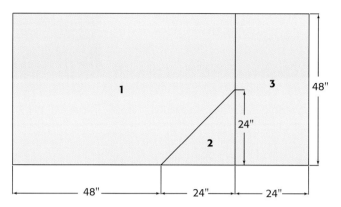

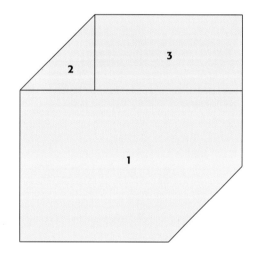

Clamping a 1 x 4 the width of your saw's foot away from the cutting line will make a good guide to make a straight cut with a circular saw. Use this same plan for cutting the foam, but use a knife so you don't melt it.

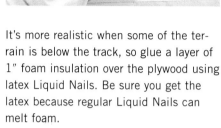

It's more realistic when some of the terrain is below the track, so glue a layer of 1" foam insulation over the plywood using latex Liquid Nails. Be sure you get the latex because regular Liquid Nails can melt foam.

To hold the foam while it dries, I screwed it down with drywall screws, which I ran in until they were about ¼" below the surface of the foam. Then I weighted the whole surface down with boxes of old MRs. As you can see, I've already started to trace out where the track will go.

ROADBED AND TRACK

With the foam in place, draw the track plan full-size on the foam. Then pin the switches in place and lay out the flextrack between them. Don't cut the flextrack yet; you're just making sure that all the track flows smoothly between the turnouts. You want to be careful with flextrack not to "cheat" and make too sharp a curve.

Before securing the track to the layout, I drew in the sawmill log pond and where the bridge would go. For the bridge, I cut through the foam and the plywood using a jigsaw. Cut right next to the unloading track for the log pond. I used a utility knife to cut the outline of the pond into the foam, then scraped it off the plywood.

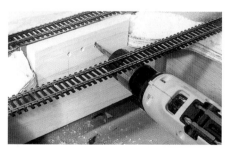

To make the dam which supports the log-dump track, fasten a piece of 1 x 4 to the edge of the plywood under the track. The overflow pipes are made from large drinking straws, which are about two feet in diameter in HO scale. Simply drill a hole and glue in a straw. The pipes should protrude about two scale feet.

As a guide, I drew lines on either side of my track while I had it in place, but you can just use your center line. Run about a three-foot bead of latex Liquid Nails at a time along a track line, and spread it with a putty knife.

I used unsplit N gauge cork roadbed. This way it's exactly the width of the HO track. Because I left it unsplit, I formed curves by snipping off short pieces with scissors and pinning it in place while the glue set.

Check that the roadbed is smooth; sand it to remove any bumps. Start laying track by gluing one turnout in place with latex Liquid Nails under the ties ahead of the frog. Don't put any glue under the moving parts.

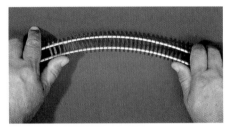

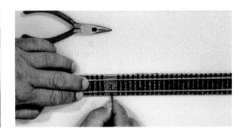

To bend flextrack, grasp firmly at the center of the piece, and bending gently, slowly work your hands first to one end, then the other. It may take several passes to get the desired radius. Trim the rail ends square with a rail nipper or motor tool and file smooth.

Remove the ties from the last ½" of track and slip on rail joiners as described below. Slide the track onto the end of the turnout and solder the joint; when it cools, file the rails smooth. The inside of the rail must be absolutely smooth to prevent derailments.

A couple dabs of latex Liquid Nails along the roadbed is plenty to hold the track in place. Where pieces of track connect you'll need to put the ties you removed back under the joint. File the ties thinner so they fit easily under the rail joiners.

At some point you'll have to fit a piece of track between two pieces already glued in place. Shape the piece but don't cut it to length. Solder it at one end and let the other end overlap the track that's in place.

Mark the overlapping track where it needs to be trimmed. Gently flex it away from the track that's attached and cut to length with a motor tool or track nipper. Clean up the ends and slip on rail joiners.

Push the rail joiners all the way onto the piece of track and it should drop into place. Now push the joiners onto the turnout rails with a pair of needlenose pliers, and solder the joints.

My father made this handy tool for spreading rail joiners. It's a piece of rail soldered into a brass tube with the base of the rail filed to a point. Push back the ties at the end of the flextrack, open up rail joiners on the tool, then slip one onto each rail and crimp in place.

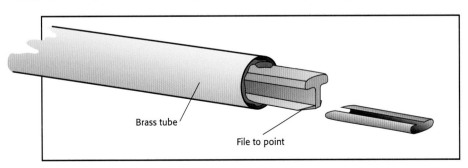

Brass tube

File to point

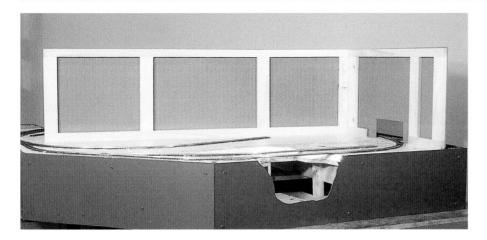

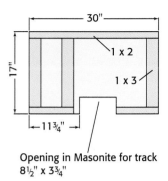

Opening in Masonite for track
8½" x 3¾"

The last step is building the scenic divider. I wanted it as thin as possible, so the frame is 1 x 2s and 1 x 3s set on their narrow dimension. When the frame was completed, I drilled through the 1 x 2s into the plywood and attached the divider with 4" screws. Sheath one side of the frame in ⅛" Masonite, then mark the hole for the mainline tunnel. Remove the divider. Cut the hole and a matching one in the sheathing for the other side. Replace the divider and sheath the other side.

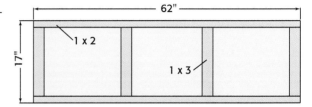

Alan Fennell assembled lots of lumber loads for me, so I named the paper mill after him.

Scenery ideas

For the final stages of the scenery, I relied heavily on Matt Coleman's book *Trains, Tracks and Tall Timber,* which is part of the Walthers Trees and Trains series. Although we often think of western scenery as rocky, the book shows that rock outcroppings were pretty rare around sawmills, so you'll see only a few on the Northwest Timber Co. I always build my scenery from back to front to avoid messing up completed work. Avoid neatness or regularity in the form and shape of the mountains or hills. I outline how far out each hill should come from the backdrop and then cut ragged pieces of foam insulation to build up the mountains.

While working on the large backdrop on my own Allegheny & Lackawanna Southern, I stumbled upon an effective yet extremely simple method of painting light summer clouds. On top of two coats of the original sky blue, I randomly brush on a roughly 50-50 mixture of white and blue across the sky. The result is a simple, fast, and realistic sky backdrop. This shot also shows the staging area which received just enough scenery to allow it to function as part of the layout.

Scenery for the Northwest Timber Co.

The Strang family adds wiring, scenery, & structures to finish our HO project railroad

By Lionel Strang | Photos by the author

We'll start with the wiring so we can get our trains running and be sure all the track is working properly before beginning the scenery.

To avoid short circuits on our layout, we need to install gaps between some of our rail sections. The track diagram shows where these are needed. You can purchase insulating rail joiners; however, as the figures show, I prefer to lay all my track in place, then cut gaps in the rails with a cutting disk. I then glue a sliver of styrene in the gap with cyanoacrylate adhesive (CA) and file the styrene to the shape of the rail.

Because I chose the MRC Command 2000 DCC (Digital Command Control) system, I didn't have to add blocks to get multiple train operation, but I made four so that if a problem arose, I could trace it more easily.

You can wire the railroad just as I did and use a standard power pack and keep one train in staging while running the other.

Finishing touches

My scenery techniques borrow a little from all the standard methods and I think produce a very nice finished project. The fun part of completing any project layout is adding the details—the finishing touches that make each scene come to life.

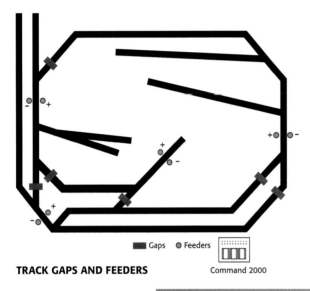

Gaps ■ Feeders ● Command 2000

TRACK GAPS AND FEEDERS

Track blocks and feeders

Gap both rails at locations indicated by heavy bars on the diagram. Because I soldered every rail joint and this is a small layout, I ran just one set of feeders to each block. Feeder wires run from the track to the terminal strips (see wiring schematic) attached to the frame between the control panel and the Command 2000 controller.

Keep track of the polarity by two different colors of feeder wire (red and black are common choices). Altogether you'll need about 50 feet of single-conductor no. 22 wire for the feeders and panel wiring.

Using pinstriping tape made for radio-control airplanes, I made a schematic of the track plan on the fascia near the controller. The shape needn't be precise as long as you can identify the tracks. I marked the block dividers with red striping and drilled ⅜" holes in each block for the SPST (on-off) switches. Mount the switches and attach the feeders.

Now is the time to run some trains and identify any track problems. Peter is using the add-on Walkaround 2000. This unit can plug into the back of the Command 2000, or you can run modular phone jacks to several points on the fascia.

WIRING DIAGRAM

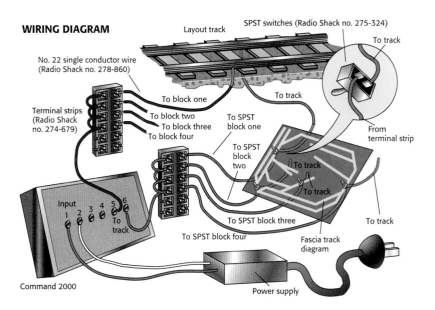

Wiring schematic

I used an old HO power pack as my power supply, but you can also purchase a transformer as described in the instructions for the Command 2000. I used Radio Shack six-position terminal strips (though I only used four positions) to split the output from the Command 2000 to each of my blocks. This same wiring scheme will work with a regular power pack.

Gap the rails in the locations shown in the wiring diagram by cutting through the rails and then gluing .020″ styrene into the gaps. File the filler pieces flush with the rails. They'll disappear when the rails are painted.

Use a ⅛″ bit to drill the holes for the feeder wires; it should be long enough to go through the foam and plywood table-top. Now push no. 22 feeder wires through the holes; use a different color for each rail.

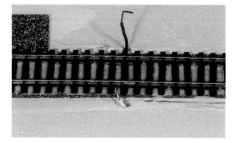

Bend the ends of the feeders 90 degrees, and solder the wires to the outside of the rails. Use a soldering gun or large (75-watt or higher) iron so that you can make the joint quickly and not melt the ties.

BALLAST

Mix up a blend of Woodland Scenics Medium and Fine Gray ballast. Spoon the ballast between the rails and spread it out with a dry brush. Because my N gauge roadbed is just the width of the ties, I could get an uneven edge, appropriate for a lightly traveled logging line.

Next, saturate the ballast with water mixed with a drop or two of liquid dish-washing detergent. I sprayed it on with an old non-aerosol hair spray bottle, but anything that gives a fine mist will do. If the water beads up and doesn't penetrate, you need a bit more detergent.

Glue the ballast with a 50-50 mix of white glue and water using a bottle with a very small opening (the top of a regular Elmer's bottle works well) so that it comes out in a very small stream or droplets. Be careful not to clog the switch points or frogs.

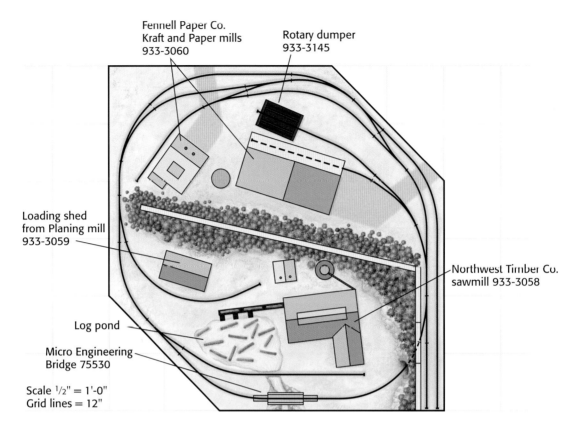

Fennell Paper Co.
Kraft and Paper mills
933-3060

Rotary dumper
933-3145

Loading shed
from Planing mill
933-3059

Northwest Timber Co.
sawmill 933-3058

Log pond

Micro Engineering
Bridge 75530

Scale ½" = 1'-0"
Grid lines = 12"

An early snow has dusted the landscape as Northwest Timber Co. no. 198 spots a string of empties at the sawmill on the Strang family's HO scale layout.

ROCKS AND HILLS

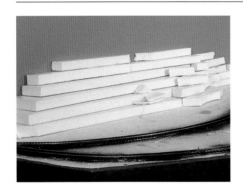

Stay within your guidelines as you build up the hills. I airbrushed my track with Floquil Rail Brown (you could use an aerosol can) and then added a light coat of Weathered Black. Don't get paint on the points of the switches. When dry, clean the top of the rail.

Secure the foam with small amounts of latex Liquid Nails. Cover it with a layer of industrial strength paper towels dipped into a soupy mixture of Hydrocal (a lightweight but strong plaster available in hobby shops and from industrial suppliers).

I made my rock molds from tin foil. Take about a 6" x 10" piece, lightly crumple it, open it up, and turn up the edges so it forms a shallow bowl. Now pour in Hydrocal mixed to a gravy-like thickness. After about five minutes, lay the mold in the desired location on the mountain.

TREES

Making all the trees we'd need to represent the Pacific Northwest wasn't so bad. First cut the filters into three or four different size squares, ranging from ½" to 2" square.

Round off the squares. Then dip a bamboo skewer in white glue and push the squares onto it. Start with a 2" square for the bottom branches and work down in size.

We stuck the trees in a leftover piece of foam and let them dry overnight. The next day I spray-painted them dark green.

As soon as you finish spraying paint, sprinkle Woodland Scenics ground foam, either Green Grass or Weeds, onto the still-wet paint to give a more realistic texture and add color highlights to the trees.

To plant the trees, simply punch holes in the plaster shell with a screwdriver and stick the trees into the foam underneath. Under the trees, I spread a very thin covering of poly fiber and spray it green.

Here we see Alan Fennell blowing on a mixture of Woodland Scenics Green Grass and Weeds over the poly fiber after he'd soaked it with diluted glue. The poly fiber gave the area an overgrown look.

ROCKS AND HILLS

Peter is staining the casting with a mix of dry tempera paints and water, which are readily available at art supply stores. We used just black and burnt umber. Apply the stain lightly, let dry, then restain to darken it as you deem necessary.

Add ground texture by applying a liberal coating of glue and water, then blowing on a mixture of Woodland Scenics Grass and Earth. Let it dry overnight and then vacuum off the excess. Paint areas without rock castings a dark green as a base coat.

On the Northwest Timber Co. side of the layout we used the sawmill, slash burner, and loading shed. Once I'd finished this scene I realized the loading shed seemed a bit lonely, so I might go back and add the planing mill as a shallow relief building (basically just use one long wall) right behind it.

I built up the sawmill (more on structures in a minute) so that I could decide exactly where the mill and the conveyor would sit in relation to the log pond. I supported the conveyor legs that go in the pond with a small block of wood.

Before I filled the pond with a gravy-like mixture of Hydrocal, I made sure that the bottom was completely sealed so there'd be no leaks. I placed logs cut from small pine branches in the wet plaster, leaving the top halves of them exposed.

Because I wanted to make dirty looking water typical of log ponds, I poured Woodland Scenics Earth into the rest of the exposed Hydrocal. Then I soaked the turf with water and applied a 50-50 glue and water mixture to secure it.

After the plaster and earth has dried, install the log conveyor, making sure it touches the surface of the pond. Apply a coat of artist's acrylic gloss medium.

To simulate the water that runs out of the culverts, I put a piece of scotch tape from each culvert to the ground and coated it with acrylic gloss gel. Once the gel dried, I dry-brushed the water a greenish brown.

I built the Micro-Engineering kit per instructions, but then glued the bridge to the bottom of the flextrack that was already in place. When set, I installed the trestle bents.

Setting the scene

All the structures are from the Walthers Trees and Trains series and the bridge is from Micro-Engineering. Build the structures, then experiment with their exact placement. You may then want to go in and add most of the ground cover, then reinstall the buildings, and finish up by adding roads and touching up the ground cover.

I named the main mill for my friend Alan Fennell, who assembled all those wood pallets being loaded at the sawmill. I built a paved road for the paper mill and a dirt one for the kraft mill.

I used a very thick mix for the road and formed the edges freehand. Before the plaster set, I used an old set of trucks to make the flangeways next to the rails. Later, I cleaned these flangeways with a knife and file.

I formed the parking lot and road for the dirt drive at the kraft mill in the same manner as the paved ones, except I covered it with a fine-grained sand I found behind my house. You could use any of the commercial dirt and rock products.

For most of the flat areas, I simply spread out matte medium with a wet brush, and then sprinkled on various shades of ground foam. Much of the Pacific Northwest is downright swampy, so in some areas I substituted gloss medium.

The rotary dumper kit arrived after we'd almost finished the layout, but changes are easy to make. I just drilled holes at the corners where I needed the opening and joined them using a saber saw.

Winnepesaukee Central

An HO scale project layout to
demonstrate scenery techniques

By George Sebastian-Coleman | Photos by Jim Forbes

Do a video on scenery! That's the problem with success: They want you to repeat it. After our video on airbrushing, it seemed sensible to do another and scenery seemed a natural subject. We debated shooting it on our home layouts but felt the logistics would be unwieldy and that in the end there'd be no unified scene to point at and say, "See how great that looks and it really wasn't that much work."

So we built a project layout instead, which we think looks great, and it was only a wee bit more work than we'd planned on.

Concept and track plan

Marty McGuirk drew the track planning assignment. Not surprisingly, we ended up in New England with a railroad name only he could pronounce (WIN-a-puh-SAW-key). Operations wasn't the main design issue, but we still wanted the finished layout to be usable. For scenic demonstrations we wanted one rural scene with both a fast-moving creek and a large, still body of

The *Model Railroader* staff built this HO scale layout to demonstrate scenery techniques on our new videotape, "Model Railroad Scenery Made Easy." It's available at your local hobby shop, or order direct at 800-533-6644.

water, and a town to show making roads and blending structures into the scene. Walthers had just released its covered bridge, and nothing says New England like a covered bridge, so the creek side of the layout pretty much designed itself. The town side has two signature industries—a textile mill and a marble quarry—and don't forget those dairy cows!

Benchwork

Keeping things simple, we had the lumberyard cut four eight-foot 1 x 4s and two eight-foot 2 x 2s in half. We also ordered three six-foot pieces of 1 x 4 (two for the long sides and one for risers). The cross

The afternoon local rolls through the town of Winnepesaukee. Jeff Wilson made the roads using sheet styrene.

Note how the Walthers Midstate Marble Works is built up on higher ground so the spur descends into the loading area.

and screwed it in). To provide support for risers at the middle of each end, I added two more joists between the end piece and the next cross-member.

Thanks in part to the precut lumber, I was able to assemble the benchwork, add the roadbed, glue the track in place, hook up temporary feeders, and have a train running in only six hours. Permanent wiring was only a matter of adding a bus wire from the feeders on one side of the layout to those on the other side. If I were wiring this for home use, I'd gap the passing sidings as shown on the track plan and add SPST switches so I could park a train either in front of the station while switching on the inside, or park the switcher and run the through train.

Rural Winnepesaukee

A variety of scenery techniques was the name of the game, so to the covered bridge's right is Slab Mountain, which Marty built from layers of rigid foam insulation. Across the creek, Jim Kelly built Web Hill with the time-tested cardboard-strip supports covered with plaster gauze and Sculptamold.

I cast the rockwork for the creek bed in latex molds, applying some wet and gluing others in place. Jim Kelly built the embankment along the lake from real limestone, and Jim Hediger carved sedimentary rocks on the other corner. Marty poured the creek using Enviro-Tex epoxy resin while Jeff Wilson made the lake with gloss acrylic medium.

Andy Sperandeo demonstrated basic ground cover using ground foam from Woodland Scenics and Scenic Express. He made weeds using Woodland Scenics Field Grass. Melanie Buellesbach built the trees using the tree armatures and netting from Accurail's new Easy-Scene line of scenery materials, with greenery provided by Woodland Scenics ground foams (Easy-Scene foliage was not available yet).

bracing is ¼″ x 1⅛″ rectangular molding. The resulting frame is 4′-1½″ wide and 6′-0″ long, since the halved 1 x 4s were put between the six-foot stringers.

Even though the roadbed is completely level, we put it up on risers to demonstrate that there should be as much scenery below track level as there is above it.

We used Atlas True-Track, which has built-in roadbed. When I laid out Marty's plan on a sheet of ¾″ plywood I realized that the spur to the mill turned too sharply, cutting into the area for the creek side of the layout. True-Track doesn't have

as many available pieces as Snap-Track, so I cut down a curved section to a one-third size, using a Snap-Track piece as my guide. This meant the cut end of the piece did not snap into place, but this wasn't a problem as the rail joiners aligned it. I glued all the track to the plywood with Liquid Nails for Projects.

After laying out the track, I traced around it on the plywood and cut out my roadbed using a saber saw. I then cut risers to raise the track roadbed about 4″ above the benchwork (I took one piece of 1 x 4 and laid it on the cross-members and aligned the top of the riser with that

Industrial Winnepesaukee

Walthers Midstate Marble Works and Ertl's Easton Mill provided the two on-line industries. I built the marble works and overhead crane on a base of .060″ styrene. The ground was built up before installing the building so the spur is recessed, allowing the crane to travel over a car spotted on the spur.

Still trying to keep the workload down, we ordered one of Ertl's pre-built mills, but they were out of stock. The kit version proved more challenging than we'd expected and it squeaked into place the night before the final taping.

The Atlas station was liberated from the darkness under the benchwork of the Milwaukee, Racine & Troy (Kalmbach's club layout). It had served a long and useful life on the MR&T in our old building downtown, but had not found a home on the new version.

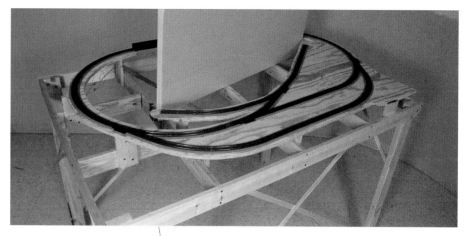

ABOVE: The benchwork is simplicity itself, precut 1 x 4s glued and screwed into a basic rectangle, with 2 x 2s bolted into the corners for legs. The backdrop is a piece of 2″-thick rigid foam insulation.

LEFT: To provide a more gentle bend for the mill spur, I used a razor saw to cut the Atlas True-Track to match an Atlas Snap-Track ⅓ curve. The cut piece is installed and the master sits in front of it.

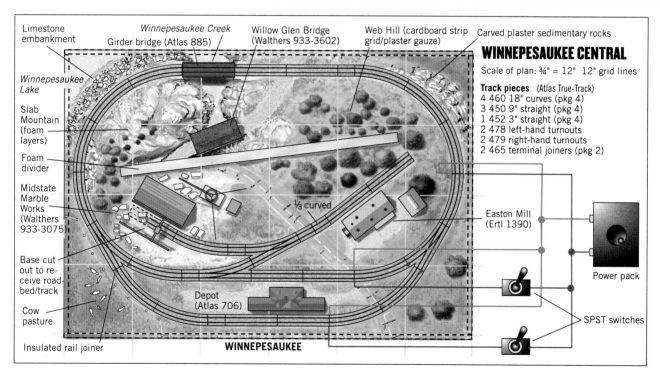

Limestone embankment

Winnepesaukee Creek
Girder bridge (Atlas 885)

Willow Glen Bridge (Walthers 933-3602)

Web Hill (cardboard strip grid/plaster gauze)

Carved plaster sedimentary rocks

WINNEPESAUKEE CENTRAL

Scale of plan: ¾" = 12" 12" grid lines

Track pieces (Atlas True-Track)
4 460 18" curves (pkg 4)
3 450 9" straight (pkg 4)
1 452 3" straight (pkg 4)
2 478 left-hand turnouts
2 479 right-hand turnouts
2 465 terminal joiners (pkg 2)

Winnepesaukee Lake

Slab Mountain (foam layers)

Foam divider

Midstate Marble Works (Walthers 933-3075)

⅓ curved

Easton Mill (Ertl 1390)

Power pack

Base cut out to receive roadbed/track

Cow pasture

Depot (Atlas 706)

SPST switches

Insulated rail joiner

WINNEPESAUKEE

The Appalachian Central

A project layout that traces its roots to the 1950s but features modern methods and materials

By Lionel Strang | Photos by the author

Welcome to the N scale Appalachian Central Ry. The roots of this project can be traced back to the time I spent flipping through some back issues of *Model Railroader* looking for information on lumber mills while building the Northwest Timber Co. During the course of my search I found the January 1950 issue, which featured a track plan for the Timberline & Tidewater by Linn Westcott.

As I studied the plan I couldn't help but wonder what kind of layout Linn—or any of his fellow modelers at the mid-point of the 20th century—could have created if they'd had modern tools and materials.

The seed for this project had been planted: Start with a good design for a small, operations-oriented layout and then show readers how to build it utilizing as many of today's products and techniques as possible.

To make it even more interesting, I chose N scale, a modeling scale unknown at the time Linn planned his T&T. The railroad is set in the Appalachian Mountains of the eastern United States and loosely based on the area around Grafton, W. Va. This was an easy choice for me since I'm familiar with that region.

Selecting an era was also an easy choice. Turn-of-the-century modeling was regularly featured in MR back in the 1950s. The AC is therefore a turn-of-the-century pike, reflecting railroading at the end of the 20th century—just after CSX acquired half of Conrail.

A modern day model railroad

While Linn's original track plan was fundamentally sound—a testimony to his design abilities—it lacked many elements we take for granted today.

There was no provision for "off the layout" destinations, no way to separate individual scenes (thereby making the layout seem larger), little provision for local switching, no provision for continuous running, and little space for scenery and structures. The AC would need all those things for me to consider it a truly up-to-date model railroad.

Of course, N scale opened up a number of possibilities for my 28.5-square foot-area that Linn could have only dreamed about.

Wiring even a simple model railroad can seem a daunting task, but today multitrain control is a snap thanks to Digital Command Control (DCC). There are so many good DCC systems that choosing one for the AC wasn't easy. After thorough investigation I chose the Digital Plus system (Set-01) from Lenz. What really sold me on this system was the easy-to-understand manual. If you follow the directions you'll be running trains in no time.

All of the locomotives, with the exception of one Kato unit, came equipped with DCC decoders. The freight cars came from all the major N scale manufacturers, although I equipped all the rolling stock with Micro-Trains couplers.

The completed layout design looks little like the T&T and features two four-track staging yards, a small classification yard, a junction, and enough operating possibilities to keep my son Peter and me busy. Not bad for less than 30 square feet.

First we'll concentrate on getting the Appalachian Central up and running. Then we'll add scenery, buildings, and the other finishing touches that make a layout a railroad.

The diagram shows how I built the benchwork and backdrop support frame. I wanted the layout to be strong and easy to transport, so I built a light wood frame and filled the open areas with foam board insulation.

I used drywall screws and a cordless screwdriver to assemble the frame, applying a small bead of carpenter's glue along each joint for added strength.

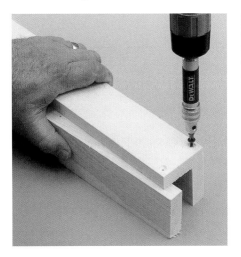

Lionel used a countersink tool to countersink the pilot holes for the screws. Here he's assembling the L girders.

Before adding the foam I built the backdrop frame. To keep the frame as stiff as possible I screwed metal L brackets to each of the inside corners.

I assembled the legs as shown in the drawing, making the legs 42" long. I wanted the layout to be rather tall because I've found the closer N scale trains are to eye level the more realistic they appear.

Whenever possible add a thin bead of carpenter's glue to provide added strength to the frame.

Drywall screws, installed using a cordless screwdriver, make benchwork assembly go very quickly.

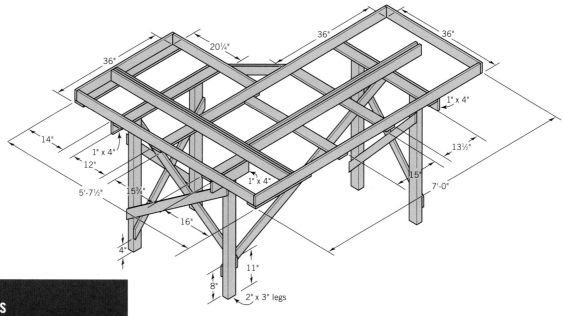

Bill of materials

Benchwork
1 x 3 lumber, 10 feet long (13)
2 x 3 lumber, 4 feet long (6)
1 x 4 lumber, 10 feet long (1)
1" foam board, 4 x 8 sheet (4)
1½" foam board, 4 x 8 sheet (4)
.060" styrene, 4 x 8 sheet (1)
¼" Masonite, 4 x 8 sheet (1)

Atlas
92500 30" flextrack (28)
92510 9¾"-radius curve (11)
92520 11"-radius curve (6)

Kato
20434 through truss bridge (2)

Lenz
01 Digital Plus Digital Command Control system

Peco Insulfrog turnouts
1734 curved right turnout (3)
1735 curved left turnout (4)
1738 right turnout, medium (12)
1739 left turnout, medium (5)
1741 wye (1)

Woodland Scenics
1410 incline set, 2 percent
1412 incline starter, 2 percent
1444 foam tack glue (2)
1462 track-bed bulk pack (2)

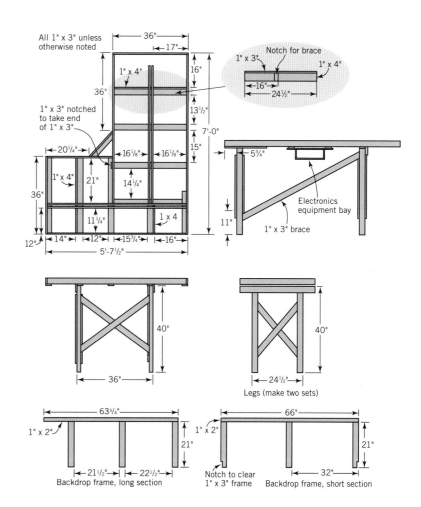

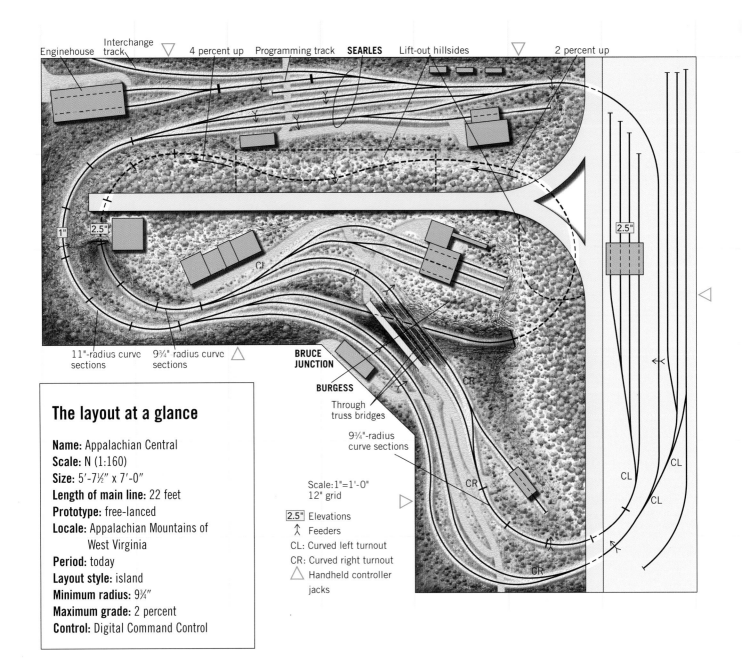

Enginehouse — Interchange track — 4 percent up — Programming track — **SEARLES** — Lift-out hillsides — 2 percent up

1" — 2.5"

2.5"

11"-radius curve sections — 9¾" radius curve sections

BRUCE JUNCTION

BURGESS

Through truss bridges

9¾"-radius curve sections

CR

CR

CR

CL

CL

CL

CL

2.5"

The layout at a glance

Name: Appalachian Central
Scale: N (1:160)
Size: 5'-7½" x 7'-0"
Length of main line: 22 feet
Prototype: free-lanced
Locale: Appalachian Mountains of West Virginia
Period: today
Layout style: island
Minimum radius: 9¾"
Maximum grade: 2 percent
Control: Digital Command Control

Scale:1"=1'-0"
12" grid

2.5" Elevations
⋏ Feeders
CL: Curved left turnout
CR: Curved right turnout
△ Handheld controller jacks

ADDING THE FOAM BOARD

Most of the flat surfaces of the AC are foam board, a building insulation material also commonly called blue or pink board. The color does not matter for our purposes.

Always use only water-based adhesives with foam board since solvent-based glues will dissolve the foam. I used yellow carpenter's glue for all the wood-to-foam board joints. While this took a little longer to dry than some other adhesives it produces an incredibly strong bond.

I allowed the first layer of foam (the 1½" piece) to dry overnight and the next day put a liberal coat of yellow glue on it, placed the 1" on top, and again waited overnight. If you're careful while cutting the foam you'll only need four 1½" sheets and four 1" sheets to fill the frame.

Lionel used yellow carpenter's glue to bond the foam board together. Here he's spreading the glue with a disposable brush.

INSTALLING THE BACKDROP

While the backdrop is more scenic than structural it's a good idea to install it now rather than waiting and risking damage to track and structures.

The backdrops are made from a 4 x 8-foot sheet of .060″ styrene, cut 24″ wide. The styrene is supported by wood frames. To fasten the styrene to wood I used a water-based contact cement, which worked very well.

You can purchase large sheets of styrene from wholesale plastic suppliers (check the Yellow Pages under "Plastics"). Cut the styrene by scribing a line with a utility knife, bend it along the scribe, and the styrene will snap.

I used Quick-Grip clamps to hold the styrene while the cement dried. The next morning I trimmed away any excess with a sharp utility knife.

The roadbed is Woodland Scenics Track-Bed, a fairly new product made of a light, pliable foam which is much lighter and less messy than cork.

Lionel notched the backdrop support in a couple of places. Here he's using a scrap piece of 1 x 3 to trace cut lines on the support. He then cut it out with a jigsaw.

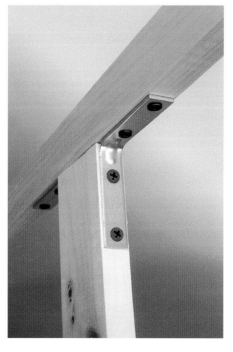

Metal L brackets help to keep the backdrop frame rigid. These are held in place with drywall screws.

To join two pieces of styrene Lionel cut a splice plate from scrap material and secured the pieces together with cyanoacrylate adhesive (CA).

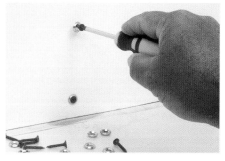

In areas that will be hidden by scenery use drywall screws to attach the backdrop to the frame.

After the cement dried Lionel carefully trimmed away any excess styrene with a utility knife.

The backdrops are supported by 1 x 3s run perpendicular to the benchwork.

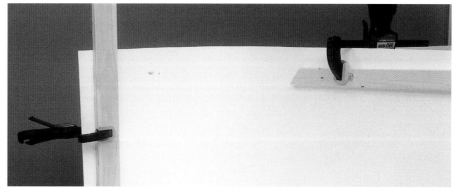

Secure the styrene backdrop to the frame with water-based contact cement and clamp it in place.

The track on the second level is 2½" above the rest of the layout to provide clearance for the bridges at Bruce Junction. I elevated the track using precut foam incline sections from Woodland Scenics Sub-Terrain system. This is an easy way to install smooth, even grades.

Each incline section is 2½" x 24" long and raises the track by ½" (2 percent grade). I used four riser sections to gain an elevation of 2" and then added a 2 percent starter on top of the fourth piece at the end of the grade to get to an elevation of 2½".

The photos show how I installed the risers and roadbed. Just be sure to apply a thin coat of adhesive since setting a riser in a big glob of glue can throw the incline off kilter—and make the grade steeper than you want.

Spiking some iron

I installed the track on the lower level before installing the sub-roadbed for the upper level track. No matter what order you choose to lay the track the procedure is the same.

I used Peco Insulfrog turnouts with a combination of Atlas flex-track and sectional track. I decided on the Peco turnouts to keep the wiring as simple as possible since the insulated frogs mean you don't need to cut gaps in the rail. The Peco turnouts have a built-in spring to hold the points, eliminating the need for any additional mechanism.

While most of the track is flex-track I used sectional track for the three most important mainline curves. The curve leading uphill from Bruce Junction is 11"-radius sectional track. I used 9¾" curves in two locations: downhill from Burgess and leading into the upper staging yard.

On curves I used a sharp knife to cut the roadbed in half along the center line, which makes it easier to bend the roadbed to the desired curve and keep the roadbed flat.

Once the risers were in place I installed the foam for the second level. Again I used a 1½" piece and a 1" piece to make up the required 2½" thickness. I laid the track and installed the two Kato truss bridges, which are supported on Chooch cut stone abutments.

I used an airbrush to paint the track a mixture of Polly Scale Rail Brown and Tarnished Black. Cover the switch points with masking tape since paint on the points will interfere with electrical contact.

WIRING

The Appalachian Central is controlled with Lenz Digital Command Control. Like most DCC systems this one consists of a separate command station and booster. It also requires a power supply. A conventional power pack provides more than enough juice to run a small layout like the Appalachian Central.

I could have powered the layout with a single set of feeders placed between Bruce Junction and Searles, but this wouldn't be very reliable. I wired the AC as shown in the wiring diagram.

The feeders are no. 20AWG wires that have been soldered to the underside of the rails as shown in the tracklaying section.

Use the track plan to position the track on the benchwork. Trace along the outline of the ties and remove the track. Next spread Woodland Scenics Foam Tack glue between the lines.

After spreading the Foam Tack glue, Lionel positioned the roadbed, pressed down firmly, and used pushpins to hold the roadbed in place until the glue dried.

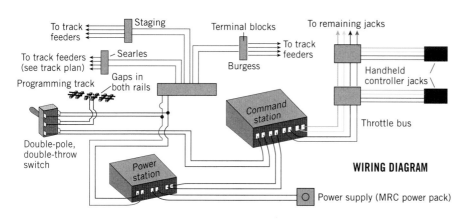

WIRING DIAGRAM

The Appalachian Central is controlled with this Lenz Digital Plus (St-01) Digital Command Control system. The power pack only provides power to the booster; it isn't used to control the trains.

Extra sections of roadbed are handy for creating a large, flat area. Lionel used several pieces of foam roadbed to support the coal mine at Burgess.

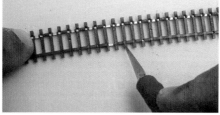

Lionel used a hobby knife to remove spacers between the ties on the underside of the flextrack. Push the ties apart to make room for feeder wires.

Lionel soldered the feeder wires in place prior to laying the track. The locations of the feeder wires are shown on the track plan of the finished layout.

The elevated track sections are supported using Woodland Scenics incline sets. Lionel held the incline sections in place and marked the edges. The T pins are used to hold the incline in place.

The incline sections are cemented in place with a thin coat of latex-based adhesive. Be sure to used only a small amount of adhesive as too much can put the risers out of kilter.

Next, Lionel laid the track, by spreading a thin layer of glue on the roadbed and holding the track in place with push pins until the glue dried. Here he's using a utility knife to trim the roadbed edges.

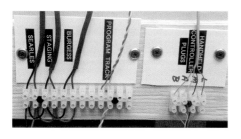

This view of the underside of the layout shows the closest thing the AC has to a "control panel."

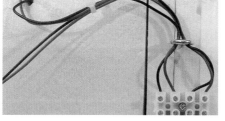

Neatness counts. The feeders go from the main terminal strip to smaller strips where they connect to feeders soldered to the underside of the rails.

Lionel used terminal blocks to connect wiring from the throttle bus connection, located on the command station, to the throttle jacks located around the layout.

Scenery for the Appalachian Central

We conclude our N scale project layout with ballast, scenery, and structures

By Lionel Strang | Photos by the author

Last chapter, I introduced the N scale Appalachian Central, a modern layout which was designed to use modern materials and techniques. At the end of Part 1 we had the benchwork built, had installed .060″ styrene backdrops, and all the track was laid. We had also installed the Lenz Digital Command Control system and were running trains.

But as fun as running trains on bare foam board benchwork is, you'll find nothing in model railroading is better than running trains through a realistic setting. But remember, this is a hobby, not a job. Ballast some track, add a few trees to a hillside, or build a structure as the mood strikes.

Forty years ago realistic model railroad scenery was unheard of. There were virtually no commercial scenery products and the prevailing techniques often produced less than stunning results. Happily, that situation has radically changed and it's now possible for almost anyone to produce satisfying scenery.

BALLASTING

I ballasted the track with Woodland Scenics fine ballast, one bag of light gray and two bags of gray, mixing the three bags together in a bowl to vary the color somewhat. I spread the ballast onto the track with a teaspoon and then used a spreader to even it out.

After spreading the ballast, I sprayed it with water with a couple of drops of detergent added to reduce the surface tension. This helps the bonding agent of a 1:1 mixture of white glue and water soak into the ballast.

After spreading the ballast Lionel uses a mini-vac nozzle on his Shop-Vac to remove loose ballast from around the switch points.

Spray the ballast with "wet" water, soaking it completely.

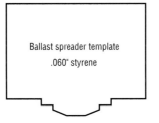

Ballast spreader template
.060" styrene

ABOVE LEFT AND ABOVE RIGHT: Lionel used a styrene spreader to even out the ballast and create a realistic slope.

RIGHT: Secure the ballast with a mixture of white glue and water.

SCENERY

Lionel built the mountains by gluing foam board in place "wedding cake" fashion. He then shaped the foam with a hot wire tool.

Lionel left two lift-out sections (see track plan) for access to the branch line. Here's the access hatch at Burgess.

After the mountains have been forested the hatch is hidden, but when the hatch is removed, as shown here, it's easy to reach hidden track.

Scenery is my favorite part of the hobby so I was anxious to get started. The mountains are foam board pieces stacked like a wedding cake. I started by making a paper template for the bottom of each mountain. Then I traced the template onto the foam board and cut it out with a utility knife.

Once satisfied the first piece fit, I used it as a template and traced its outline on a second piece of foam. Then I cut the second piece 1" inside the outline. Next I used the second piece as an outline for the third, again cutting 1" inside the line, continuing this process until the mountain was the correct height. When finished the mountain should look like a three-dimensional contour map or an inedible wedding cake.

I glued the layers together with Sticks-a-Foam, a special adhesive specifically designed for foam board, which I purchased from Home Depot. Once the cement dried I shaped the mountains with a hot wire foam cutter.

A word of warning: Always use the foam cutter in a well-ventilated area as the fumes are unhealthy. Also, foam cutters vary in price and quality. I started with a cheaper version which didn't work properly and was taking too much time and effort. In an attempt to preserve my sanity, I reinvested in a more expensive model from Hot Wire Foam Factory and found it worked like a charm. Good tools are always worth the extra money.

There were two locations, shown on the track plan, where I added lift-out sections of foam to access the branchline tracks. The foam mountains made it easy to create these lift-out sections.

PAINTING THE BACKDROP

Lionel painted most of the backdrop with blue and white flat latex paint. Keeping the sky lighter by adding more white near the bottom and applying more blue as you work toward the top gives the backdrop more depth.

Lionel used stencils from New London Industries to add hills and clouds to the backdrop behind the staging yard. For the hills he held the stencil against the backdrop and painted it with various shades of green.

For the clouds Lionel held the stencil a couple of inches away from the backdrop and sprayed it with white spray paint. Holding the stencil away from the backdrop gave the clouds a softer edge.

Years ago I realized you don't have to be an artist to paint a realistic sky behind a layout. I use light sky blue color and white flat latex paint, painting it by dipping the brush first into the blue and then into the white paint, adding just a little white to the blue. When you paint the backdrop you'll end up with a sky that looks like a hazy summer day. Near the top of the backdrop make the blue more intense by adding less white. Closer to the ground add a bit more white. This creates a nice cloudless sky.

Following the suggestion of my friend Paul Burgess I decided to leave the staging yard unscenicked. At first I painted the backdrop the same as the rest of the layout but without any scenery the staging area looked really dull. At the 1999 National Model Railroad Association convention in St Paul, Minn., I discovered cloud and hill stencils from New London Industries in San Antonio, Texas. These stencils create different background scenes for model railroads. I chose to use the low hills and cloud stencils.

TREE-COVERED HILLSIDES

Once the mountains were complete I painted them with dark green latex paint. Modeling Appalachian mountainsides with individual trees would take far too long. Instead, I opted to capture the look of tree-covered hillsides using the same technique that I used on my HO scale Allegheny & Lackawanna Southern.

I use a black poly fiber (poly fiber is a synthetic fiber) made by the Putnam Company of Walworth, Wis. This stuff is often sold for use as costume beards so try arts and crafts stores. If you can't find black poly fiber, you can spray-paint white poly fiber with inexpensive black spray paint.

The photos and captions show how I forested the layout. This process goes quickly and gives the entire railroad a finished appearance.

Lionel started making his tree-covered hillsides by brushing a liberal coat of white glue onto a 2 x 2-foot area.

Gently pull apart a clump of poly fiber until it's almost transparent. Once satisfied with how it looks place it on the mountain.

Lionel applied spray adhesive to a 12″ x 12″ area and poured some Woodland Scenics fine Green Grass and Weeds onto a folded index card and gently blew the foam onto the still-wet adhesive.

Here Lionel is adding a second layer of coarse turf. Using either Medium Green or Dark Green will give the trees some additional texture and also create the illusion of shadows in the forest canopy.

ROADS

I made the roads from fine grade mortar sand. This material, available in 25-pound bags for less than $5, is clean, dry, and ready to use.

Once the sand is leveled I bond the road in place with a mixture of one part white glue and one part water. I paint the roads with Polly Scale Tarnished Black to represent newer pavement or Grimy Black for older pavement.

Lionel drew an outline for his roads on the scenery with a marker.

Then he pours the sand between the lines and levels it with a piece of scrap styrene.

Once the sand has been spread out to form roads Lionel uses a mini-vac attachment to remove any excess.

Lionel glues the sand in place and allows it to dry overnight. Here, he's testing the flangeway clearance on a grade crossing.

Lionel used a cutoff disk in a motor tool to carefully clear some of the dried sand out of the way of wheel flanges.

GROUND COVER ROCKS, AND FASCIA

For ground cover I used a variety of materials from Woodland Scenics and Scenic Express. I painted the foam board with a liberal coat of dark green latex paint and sprinkled the first layer of ground cover onto the wet paint. I let the paint and ground cover dry overnight and the next day added a second layer of ground cover, securing it with a solution of one part white glue and one part water.

The fascia is ¼″ Masonite hardboard. Most of the fascia is 6″ high but in some spots it's taller to follow the scenery contours. Hold the Masonite against the side of the layout and trace an outline of the landscape. Cut along the marked line with a jigsaw, and screw the fascia in place. I painted the fascia with dark green latex semigloss paint.

Rather than mess with cast or carved plaster rock outcroppings, which would also added weight to the layout, I carved the rock strata into the foam board hills. The photos show how I made these easy foam rocks.

RIGHT: To avoid using any plaster, which would have been messy and heavy, Lionel carved rocks into the foam using a Dremel Moto-Tool.

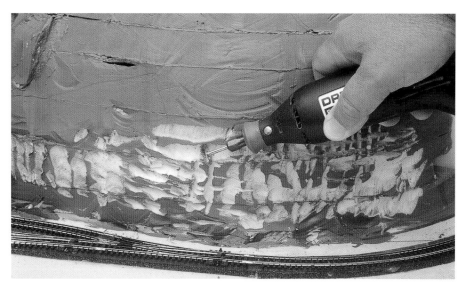

A stiff wire brush not only added some finer strata, it also cleaned the foam crumbs from the hillside.

Lionel painted the "rocks" with inexpensive acrylic paints. He blended raw sienna, burnt umber, and raw umber.

While the paint is still wet blow on some fine ground foam for texture. Here Peter Strang demonstrates how this is done.

STRUCTURES

I used a variety of buildings on the railroad, mostly plastic kits which I painted and weathered. With hundreds of great N scale structures to choose from there was no way I could use them all. I tried to pick buildings appropriate for the region and era. The track plan identifies the ones I used.

Most of the structures are built stock although I painted and weathered everything to help blend the structures with the rest of the layout.

I got two buildings for the price of one when I added some styrene strips and extra legs to the slack loader included in the Walthers New River Mine kit to build a small coal loader for Burgess.

Lionel used the slack loader from the Walthers New River mine kit to construct this coal tipple for Burgess. He mounted the loader on legs made from Evergreen styrene shapes.

The two stations are kits. I built the freight depot from Design Preservation Models' modular wall system. Use the photos for weathering and placement ideas, but feel free to substitute buildings as you see fit.

Burgess Coal Co. Mine no. 2 is a Walthers New River Mine kit. The bridges are Kato bridges which Lionel painted and weathered and the Bruce Junction depot is a Clarksville depot, also from Walthers.

An ex-Conrail Geep, still wearing blue, works the Medusa Cement spur. The structure is a Walthers kit which Lionel painted and customized with signs made on a computer.

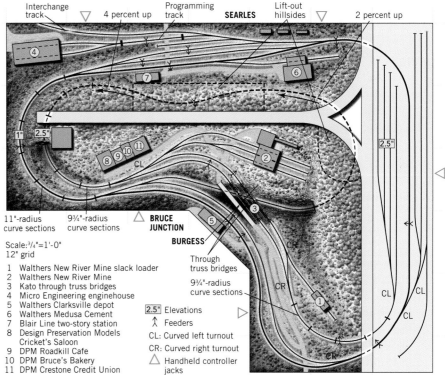

1 Walthers New River Mine slack loader
2 Walthers New River Mine
3 Kato through truss bridges
4 Micro Engineering enginehouse
5 Walthers Clarksville depot
6 Walthers Medusa Cement
7 Blair Line two-story station
8 Design Preservation Models Cricket's Saloon
9 DPM Roadkill Cafe
10 DPM Bruce's Bakery
11 DPM Crestone Credit Union

Scale: 3/4"=1'-0"
12" grid

2.5" Elevations
⋏ Feeders
CL: Curved left turnout
CR: Curved right turnout
△ Handheld controller jacks

WEATHERING THE BRIDGES, AND EVERYTHING ELSE

The twin through truss bridges are an important scenic highlight of the Appalachian Central so I wanted to make them look as good as possible, which meant improving the Kato colors with additional painting and weathering.

I discovered Bragdon Enterprises'

(2960 Garden Tower Lane, Georgetown, CA 95634) Weathering System at the Kansas City National Train Show a couple of years ago and have been using it ever since. It is much easier and faster than the more traditional weathering methods like airbrushing or thinned washes.

Abutments

I started by installing two pairs of Chooch Enterprises cut stone abutments which I weathered with a wash of water, white glue, and Polly Scale Steam Power Black, mixing two parts glue with three parts water and one part paint. Before the

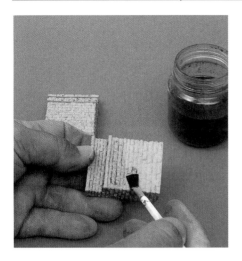
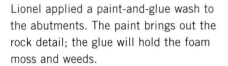

Lionel applied a paint-and-glue wash to the abutments. The paint brings out the rock detail; the glue will hold the foam moss and weeds.

Scrub the abutments with an old toothbrush. An old kit box serves to catch the excess ground foam.

TOP: The before and after shots show how a little weathering can add even more realism to an already detailed part.

ABOVE: The 8"-square strip styrene framing for the highway bridge aligns with the posts on the Central Valley fencing used as a railing.

LEFT: Excess weathering powder falls into the box for reuse. Lionel weathered the floor of the vehicle bridge with Light and Medium Rust, with a final layer of Soot to simulate oil and rubber build up.

paint and glue mixture dried I sprinkled some Woodland Scenics ground foam onto the abutment to simulate the weeds, grass, and dirt that always accumulate on old abutments and piers. After allowing everything to dry overnight I lightly scrubbed the excess foam away with an old toothbrush.

Bridges

I began work on the bridges by removing the Unitrack connectors from the rails and gently pulling the rail out of the bridge.

After the rail was removed I added a one-lane vehicle bridge running the length of one of the bridges, reminiscent of a bridge near Thurmond, W. Va. I built the vehicle bridge using V-groove sheet styrene for the floor and 8"-square strip styrene for the supporting frame. The railings are from Central Valley.

I wanted a weathered silver bridge, which is the reason I started with black bridges even though Kato offers a silver version. I painted both bridges with a mixture of two parts Polly Scale Flat Aluminum and one part SF Silver and put the bridge aside to dry.

The Weathering System is a blend of nontoxic, nonmagnetic rust, pigment, and dry adhesive. The only drawback is the stuff is very messy—in other words don't wear your Sunday best when using it.

I applied the powder with an inexpensive brush, first dipping the brush into the powder and scrub-

bing it into the surface of model. The friction of the scrubbing action activates the dry adhesive. Do this over a cardboard box to catch any excess powder which can be reused.

I've used the Weathering System on everything from bridges to freight cars on the Appalachian Central and have been pleased with the results.

END OF THE LINE

This layout was a lot of fun to build and is even more fun to operate. If you decide to build the Appalachian Central don't be afraid to add, subtract, or change things to give it some of your personality.

The Arkansas & Missouri

Background for a new
N scale layout you can build

By Mark Watson | Photos by the author

The Arkansas & Missouri has a great deal of appeal because it's a modern railroad that, well, doesn't seem so modern. Take solid consists of colorful Alcos, add mountain scenery, small towns and larger cities, a tunnel, and tall bridges, and the A&M is a railroad that simply begs to be modeled.

Goals

I wanted this project to be a good example of what can be done in two years on an average budget. I did all of the work myself, along with raising a family, buying a house, changing jobs, and dealing with other things that go on in life. For the A&M the first thing to do was to gather all the information I could find.

So in the fall of 1995 three Northern boys headed down south to soak up the local atmosphere.

A quartet of Alco C-420s blasts out of the tunnel and heads through Winslow on the N scale Arkansas & Missouri project layout.

Track plan

The track plan concentrates on the southern portion of the line from Springdale, Ark., to Van Buren, Ark., with an emphasis on the mountains. I made provisions for continuous running as well as a small visible staging yard (labeled as Fort Smith).

The plan is basically a shelf layout with larger areas on both ends for broad curves. I tried to hide the sharpest curves with either structures or trees. The ruling grade is a steep 6 percent, which is for the most part hidden on both ends by hills and trees. Track elevation ranges from 54″ at Winslow to 48″ at Springdale and Van Buren.

Wiring is cab control with two walkaround throttles. This limits the layout to two operators.

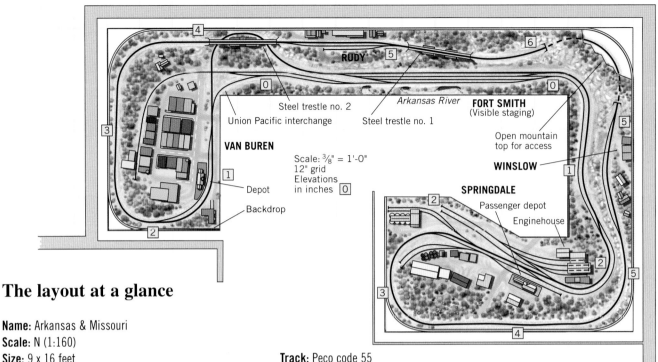

The layout at a glance

Name: Arkansas & Missouri
Scale: N (1:160)
Size: 9 x 16 feet
Locale: southwest Missouri and northwest Arkansas
Era: present
Layout height: 48″ to 54″
Layout style: along-the-walls shelf
Benchwork: open grid
Roadbed: AMI Instant Roadbed

Track: Peco code 55
Turnout minimum: no. 8
Minimum radius: 10″
Maximum grade: 6 percent
Scenery construction: Sculptamold over foam board
Backdrop: brush-painted on ⅛″ Masonite hardboard
Control: dual cab

Now it's time to start construction. I decided to use box-type construction for the layout base, supported by angle bracing attached to vertical wall supports.

The first step is making the vertical wall supports, built much like a wall in a house as fig. 1 shows. The vertical studs, which run from floor to ceiling on 16″ centers, also double as the backdrop supports.

Select the smallest wall to start. Measure the length of the wall and cut 2 x 4 headers and footers to match. Lay both boards side by side on the floor and make a mark every 16″. Use a carpenter's square to draw a line ¾″ on either side of the first mark on both boards. This marks the 1½″ width of the studs.

Measure the distance from the ceiling (or bottoms of the joists) to the floor and subtract 3″. This is how long your studs need to be.

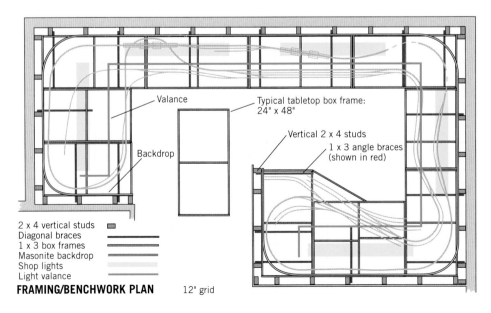

2 x 4 vertical studs
Diagonal braces
1 x 3 box frames
Masonite backdrop
Shop lights
Light valance

Valance

Backdrop

Typical tabletop box frame:
24″ x 48″

Vertical 2 x 4 studs
1 x 3 angle braces
(shown in red)

FRAMING/BENCHWORK PLAN   12″ grid

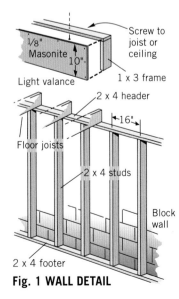

⅛″ Masonite
10″
Light valance

Screw to joist or ceiling
1 x 3 frame
2 x 4 header
16″
Floor joists
2 x 4 studs
Block wall
2 x 4 footer

Fig. 1 WALL DETAIL

Fig. 1 WALL DETAIL. Vertical studs run from floor to ceiling on 16″ centers.

Fig. 2 SPRAYING BACKDROP. Use a spray can of white paint to lightly mist the backdrop. This creates a hazy impression of distance.

Fig. 3 TREES. Use a small brush or sponge to dab paint on the near mountain forms to create the effect of trees.

Measure every 16″, because most basement floors aren't level and the distance will vary. Mark this length on the top of the bottom plate as well as on the actual stud so you can make sure you have the proper stud in the right spot.

Once all the studs are cut, assemble the frame on the floor. Place the footer on its edge and align the studs in their marked spaces. Use drywall screws through the footer to attach each stud. Repeat this with the header. When all the studs are in place, run a bead of Liquid Nails along the bottom of the footer to help secure it to the cement floor, then lift the wall into place. Make sure the bottom is firmly resting on the floor.

The final step is to screw the header to the exposed floor joists. Repeat these steps for all of the walls. This provides a strong and versatile skeleton on which to anchor the layout.

Backdrop installation

There's always a temptation to get trains running right away, but if you've ever tried to add a backdrop to an existing layout you know that the trains can wait just a bit longer. I used ⅛″ Masonite hardboard for the backdrop, saving some mess

and hassle by having the lumber-yard cut the 4 x 8-foot sheets into 2 x 8-foot pieces.

Place the hardboard all the way up to the ceiling and attach it with small finishing nails. These nails have small heads and are easily hidden. I used nails only at the very top and bottom of the backdrop, using nails in the middle only at seams.

Joint compound hides the seams of the backdrop. See fig. 1. Apply the compound with a wide putty knife and sand it smooth when it dries.

Lights and valance

I didn't want to spend a fortune on lights, but also didn't want a dark layout. A good compromise was to use standard shop light fluorescent fixtures (see the track plan for locations) but splurge and get 5100K bulbs.

To hide the light fixtures and direct most of the light onto the layout, I made valances from ⅛″ Masonite hardboard and 1 x 3 frames as fig. 1 shows. My valances hang down 10″, but you can adjust this to suit your needs.

Backdrop painting

As you can see by the photos, I painted the backdrop after adding

the angle braces, but you can learn from my mistake—it would've been easier to paint it at this point.

Paint the backdrop with a latex primer. This will give the final paint a bit of tooth to stick to and give you a true, even final color. A roller will provide an even paint coat with no brush marks.

To decide on the sky color I picked up a few blue paint swatches from the local hardware store. It's important to look at these under the lights in the layout room to get an accurate view of the color. I used America's Finest (Home Depot) no. 76-034 "shimmering sky" interior flat latex.

Once the paint dries, use a soft pencil to lightly mark the elevation of the tracks onto the backdrop. Also mark the mountain and bridge locations. This allows painting the horizon line to match the elevation of the tracks.

I've found that the most effective backdrops are usually quite simple. I used basic shapes to represent distant mountains and hills.

Artist's tube acrylics (Liquitex is one popular brand found in arts and crafts stores) work well for backdrops. I mixed various colors starting with Cadmium Yellow, Raw

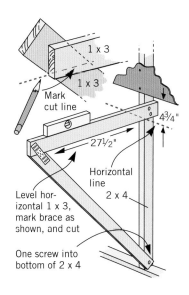

Fig. 4 BRACE. The angled braces are made from 1 x 3s as shown in the drawing above. Be sure the tops are level when installing them.

Sienna, Burnt Umber, Light Green, and Phthalocyanine Green. Start with a 1″ brush and paint the first (most distant) mountain forms a light blue-gray running the entire length of the backdrop. Using the same size brush, paint the next (closer) forms a light green.

Before putting on the next basic mountain form, I used a spray can of white paint and, standing at a distance, lightly misted the backdrop. See fig. 2. This softens the edges of the shapes and creates a hazy look, which adds to the feeling of depth.

Wait until the paint is dry and paint the next basic landscape form a grassy green. Match this to your final scenery color, which in my case was Woodland Scenics ground foam from the firm's tree kits. Matching these colors will help blend the three-dimensional foreground scenery into the two-dimensional backdrop.

I painted several small trees on the distant hills using bits of torn-up sponge dipped into greens, yellows, reds, and oranges. Simply dabbing these on the backdrop provides suitable tree shapes. Conifers can be done with a ½″ brush as in

fig. 3. I only did this to the near mountains, figuring that trees on the more distant hills would be too small to be seen. I'll wait to paint foreground trees until the basic landscape shape is finished to make sure they line up with each other.

Benchwork braces

The angular braces are held together using small flat metal truss

plates, which are hammered into the wood on either side of the angled joint as in fig. 4. Brace locations are shown on the track plan.

Make all 16 angle braces the same size. They need to extend 24″ from the edge of the studs, so the top piece is 26½″ to allow for attaching the brace to the stud.

Mark a line across all of the studs 4¾″ down from the bottom of the backdrop. This space is to accommodate the layout base. Attach a horizontal 1 x 3 to a stud at the line with a drywall screw. Use a level to check the 1 x 3 while adding another screw. With the horizontal piece secure, take a longer-than-needed 1 x 3 and attach it to the bottom of the stud with one screw. See fig. 4. Align the diagonal with the outer edge of the horizontal 1 x 3, mark it, then remove it and cut it. Use this as a pattern for cutting additional diagonal braces.

To assemble the braces, butt the pieces together on a hard surface such as a basement floor. Place the truss plate so that it's in the middle of the joint and use a hammer to nail it home. Do the same on the other side. When attaching the braces be sure to use a level to ensure that all of them will be in alignment.

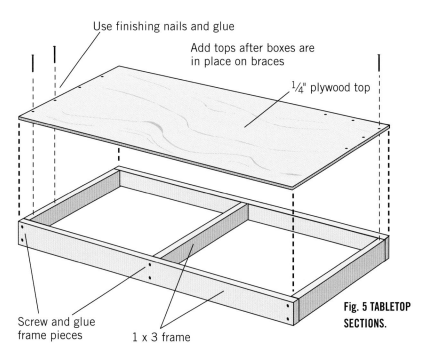

Fig. 5 TABLETOP SECTIONS.

Fig. 5 TABLETOP. The tabletop sections are simply 1 x 3 frames with ¼" plywood tops. Use drywall screws to hold them together.

Tabletop boxes

I wanted my railroad to be movable, in hopes that when we eventually move I'd be able to salvage sections of the layout. Figure 5 shows how the layout is built on a series of box frames. The track plan provides the dimensions—most are 2 x 4 feet, but a couple are different sizes.

To ensure that the butt joints were all square I used a hand miter saw and box. I glued each joint, then used 1½" drywall screws to hold them together.

The boxes rest on top of the angle braces and are screwed to each other. Just to be on the safe side I added 1 x 1 cleats in a few locations to hold the box structure to the braces.

Add a piece of ¼" plywood to the top of each box to add strength. Secure the plywood with white glue and small finishing nails.

Foam base

Add a base of 2" foam over the entire layout (don't worry about aligning joints with the boxes). I used pink extruded foam, but the blue foam will work just as well. This serves as the layout base and is the lowest level of track. The 2" thickness allows you to remove some foam to create small valleys, adding to the realism and getting away from the level "golf course" look. Another advantage of the foam base is that you can poke trees into it very easily without having to drill holes.

Transfer the entire track plan to the foam. I used the actual turnouts, held down with pins, and drew center lines with a black marker. A handy tool for drawing curves is a compass made from an old yardstick: Drill a hole at the 1" mark and insert a small nail, then drill other holes as needed.

Once all the track is marked, use a variation of the cookie-cutter method commonly used for plywood subroadbed. Cut through the foam with a serrated steak knife between the different elevations. Glue scraps of foam as risers to raise the track to the correct height. This provides a smooth grade and minimizes the number of joints. Glue a piece of foam under each joint to keep it stable. See fig. 6.

Use latex construction glue (such as Liquid Nails for Projects) to secure the foam to the top of the plywood. Use weights to hold the foam down while the glue dries (about 24 hours).

Landforms

The basic shapes of the hills and mountain are made by stacking pieces of foam as in fig. 7. Use latex Liquid Nails to hold the pieces together. The mountain top above the tunnel needs to be removable for now to allow the track to be laid. As fig. 8 shows, I made provisions to be able to reach over the top to remove derailed cars from

Fig. 6 FOAM BASE. Use scraps of foam as risers to support the upper level. The initial layers of foam can appear quite rough.

Fig. 7 BASIC LANDFORM. Stack layers of foam to create basic landforms. This is the Winslow Tunnel area.

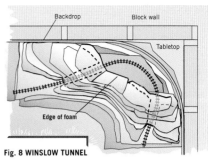

Fig. 8 WINSLOW TUNNEL

Fig. 9 CARVING TOOLS. A drywall (keyhole) saw and Stanley Surform tools of various sizes work well for shaping foam.

Fig. 10 CARVED FOAM. BELOW: Here's the tunnel area after the layers of foam have been carved to shape.

inside the tunnel after the mountain is secured.

Let the glue dry a couple of days before shaping the foam. Figure 9 shows a couple of basic tools: a handheld drywall saw to get the basic shape and a small Stanley Surform for final contouring. Figure 10 shows the completed tun-

nel area. It's messy work, as the small foam particles stick to everything. I'd suggest wearing long sleeves and using a dust mask.

A less-messy method of carving the foam is to use a hot wire tool. In a case of bad timing I got a Hot Wire Foam Factory after I had finished the majority of the carving, but I was able to use it to add the Arkansas River area in front of Fort Smith. It works really well and is very clean compared to the Surform tool. Hot-wire tools leave a very smooth finish behind, but I prefer a little rougher surface. One drawback is the smell from melted foam. Ventilate the work area as much as possible, and it's not a bad idea to wear a respirator. To meet building codes these fumes are no more toxic than wood smoke—not that that's good for you, either.

Make sure you leave room on

Fig. 11 BRIDGE AREA. Measure the length of the bridge and cut the foam base away from that area.

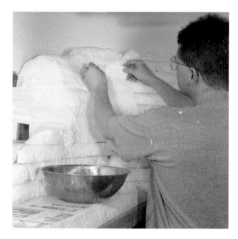

Fig. 12 PLASTER GAUZE. LEFT: Cut the gauze into small pieces. Dip each piece briefly into water, then lay it on the foam to cover any gaps.

Fig. 13 INITIAL TEXTURE. ABOVE: Sprinkle ground foam onto the wet latex paint. When the paint dries it will hold the material in place.

either side of the track center lines for the roadbed.

Foam still spanned the areas where the two tall bridges will go. I measured the two Micro Engineering kits I would be using, then used a steak knife to cut through the foam where the bridges would be. See fig. 11.

A big advantage of foam scenery is that you don't need a lot of plaster to make convincing land shapes. However, I do like to use a little plaster gauze wrap to cover any gaps that resulted from gluing layers of foam together. See fig. 12.

Give the whole layout a good cleaning using a vacuum cleaner, then wipe everything down with a damp cloth. Use 2"-wide masking tape to cover all the track center lines.

Paint the entire layout with a coat of tan latex paint. When that's completely dry, work in small sections and add a heavier coat of the same color. However, this time before the paint dries, sprinkle ground foam (I used Woodland Scenics Blended Earth Turf) over the area (fig. 13). The ground foam will stick to the wet paint and stay in place when it dries.

Fascia

The fascia is ¼" Masonite hardboard cut 12" tall. It's simply screwed onto the face of the boxes. Align the top of the fascia with the top of the 1 x 3 and not the foam. Beveling the front 2" of the foam down to the fascia makes a soft edge which helps eliminate a tabletop look. I painted the fascia semi-gloss black to make it less noticeable. (I later painted the bottom of the layout the same color.)

Trackwork for the A&M

Laying roadbed and track on our N scale
Arkansas & Missouri project layout

By Mark Watson | Photos by the author

Now we are ready to lay track on the N scale Arkansas & Missouri. I chose Peco code 55 track (meaning the railhead is .055″ above the ties) because it has a finer, more realistic appearance than the code 80 (.080″ tall) rail commonly found in N scale train sets. The Peco rail is actually a bit taller, but part of the rail is embedded in the ties, giving it strength.

The Peco code 55 flextrack comes in three-foot-long sections. The turnouts are all Peco code 55 Electrofrog no. 8 switches. The Electrofrog turnouts have the frog portion of the turnout (the V where two rails come together) live, or powered. These turnouts are power routing, meaning only one branch of the turnout is electrified at one time.

I've used these turnouts for sev-eral years and can't say enough about how much they simplify the wiring. Power routing turnouts act like toggle switches: Electricity is supplied from the point end, so whichever way the turnout is thrown is the powered route. The other route is dead (unpowered). You'll need to cut gaps in a few rails to avoid short circuits, but I'm get-ting ahead of myself.

For a track base I chose AMI Instant Roadbed. This product is made of uncured butyl rubber, meaning it's very sticky on both sides. No nails are required to hold

Complex trackwork isn't difficult to do if you take it one step at a time. This is Springdale on the N scale Arkansas & Missouri.

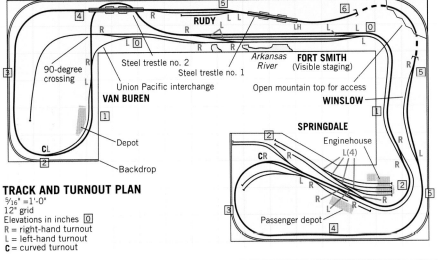

TRACK AND TURNOUT PLAN

5/16" = 1'-0"
12" grid
Elevations in inches ⓪
R = right-hand turnout
L = left-hand turnout
C = curved turnout

it in place, and the roadbed is tacky enough to hold the track securely without spikes or nails.

Getting started

To help speed tracklaying, I soldered several pairs of flextrack pieces together on my workbench. These six-foot-long sections take a bit of practice to handle, but I find they save time in installation. I also soldered together all of the groups of multiple turnouts at the workbench, as it's easier to do it there than on the layout. See fig. 1.

An added step when using AMI Instant Roadbed is to place a piece of black electrical tape along the bottom of each turnout. See fig. 2. This keeps the sticky roadbed from pushing up between the ties and fouling the switch rod (the rod connecting the points), and when we ballast track the tacky tape will hold some ballast between the ties without having to pour glue around the turnout.

Laying the roadbed

Instant Roadbed comes in rolls, with a waxed paper barrier between surfaces to keep the roadbed from sticking to itself. It comes in 1" and 2" (made for HO) widths. I used the 1" for single-track areas but 2" roadbed for sidings and the yard at Fort Smith.

The roadbed requires a smooth, clean surface to ensure good adhesion. Vacuum up any dust and then wipe the foam with a wet sponge or cloth to make sure that the surface is clean.

Take care in laying the roadbed, as once it sticks to itself it is nearly impossible to pull apart. Roll the roadbed onto the foam as in fig. 3, following the center lines we drew last month. At joints between roadbed sections, carefully butt the next piece to it. Use your finger to blend the two sections together.

After unrolling the roadbed, use a block of wood wrapped with waxed paper to press the roadbed down.

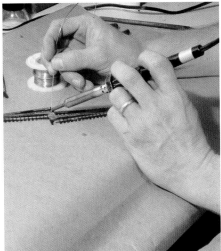

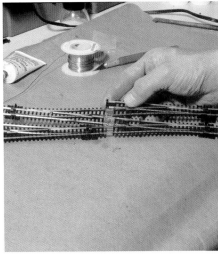

Fig. 1 SOLDERING TRACK. Solder turnout groups together before adding them to the layout. Use rosin flux (shown here in a tube and applied with a brush) to help the solder flow into the rail joints.

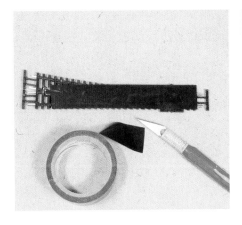

Fig. 2 PREPARING TURNOUTS. Add electrical tape to the back of each turnout, covering the throw rod as well as the ties out past the frog.

Fig. 3 LAYING ROADBED. Roll the AMI Instant Roadbed along the track center line. A wood block covered with waxed paper works well for pressing the roadbed into place.

Laying track

With the all of the roadbed stuck to the layout I began laying track. Putting down the first group of turnouts at Springdale was a great feeling—finally, track for the trains!

Take your time—trackwork needs to be done right the first time, as any problems during tracklaying will become a constant and nagging tribulation. Take a deep breath and gently lay the first turnout assembly on the roadbed, but don't press it in place yet. Instant Roadbed is tacky, but it will allow you to make adjustments if you don't press the track firmly to it. When you are positive that the track is in the correct position, then—and only then—should you press the track into the roadbed.

The flextrack will curve naturally. Bend it to shape gradually (don't attempt to create a sharp curve on the first try), then place it lightly on the roadbed so that it butts against the track section previously laid.

As fig. 4 shows, when you bend flextrack one rail will be longer than the other. Trim the longer rail to length using a rail nipper, then use a small file so that the end is square. Cut away the tie closest to the end of the track (on both ends) so that you can add rail joiners, then add the new section of track.

I soldered the rail joints as I added each new section of track. This helps keep everything aligned. When I wire the layout I'll go back and cut gaps for electrical blocks, but for now I find it easier to solder everything.

A straightedge (a steel ruler) and the old "eyeball method" were all I used to keep the flextrack straight on tangent sections. Once the track is in place and soldered it only needs a push and it's set into the roadbed for good. See fig. 5.

Bridges

I laid the Peco flextrack right over the open valleys that we created last month. The track that comes with the Micro Engineering bridge kits

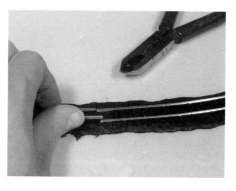

Fig. 4 TRIMMING FLEXTRACK. When bending flextrack the ends won't come out even. Use a rail nipper to trim the longer rail to length, then use a small file to make sure the end is square. When the fit is good, set the track in place with rail joiners and solder the joints.

Fig. 5 SECURING TRACK. Make sure the track is properly aligned. A firm push on the track will lock it in place on the Instant Roadbed.

has tighter tie spacing than regular flextrack. This is prototypical and looks really nice, so it's worth the little extra effort it takes to use.

Solder together enough pieces of bridge track to span each valley. Lay the bridge track atop the flextrack over the valley and mark the portion of track that needs to be cut out. Cut and remove the flextrack, then add the bridge track into place.

Final tuneup

Once all the track is in place, double-check the alignment and make sure the solder joints are smooth. Now is the time to fix the track and get it working perfectly before ballast and scenery get in the way.

Bill of materials

AMI
25 Instant Roadbed, 1" wide (3)
30 Instant Roadbed, 2" wide (1)

Atlas
2569 90-degree crossing (1)

Peco
387 RH no. 8 curved turnout (1)
388 LH no. 8 curved turnout (1)
1307 rail joiners (12 packs)
1788 RH Electrofrog no. 8 turnouts (17)
1789 LH Electrofrog no. 8 turnouts (15)
5801 flextrack (40)

This view shows the local panel at Fort Smith.

Wiring for the A&M

Cab control gets trains running on our scale project layout

By Mark Watson | Photos by the author

In choosing a control system for our N scale Arkansas & Missouri project layout, I wanted a system that would be both easy to install and easy to operate. Cab control using common-rail wiring fit the bill nicely.

Wiring intimidates a lot of people, but it really shouldn't. If you approach wiring logically and methodically, you'll have trains running in no time. Just remember that although wiring might sometimes appear complex, it's just a matter of connecting one wire at a time.

As I've gone through the stages of building the A&M I've made sure I had all the materials needed to finish each job before I started, and with wiring this is even more important. But most vital is to have all of your wiring decisions made before you strip that first wire.

Decisions

The A&M uses a relatively simple cab control system with two throttles. There are several ways to wire a layout for twin cab control, and all have their positives and negatives—pardon the pun. Cab control simply means that you'll be able to operate two trains at the same time by divid-ing the track into isolated electrical blocks (or sections) of track. Each block is controlled by a toggle switch that allows you to choose which throttle is in control of that block.

For an in-depth look at several wiring options, I strongly suggest that you pick up a copy of Andy Sperandeo's excellent book *Easy Model Railroad Wiring*, published by Kalmbach.

I decided to use common-rail wiring, meaning gaps for electrical blocks only need to be cut in one rail. The other rail is continuous and serves as a common return for both power packs. The diagram in fig. 1 shows how common-rail wiring works.

You'll also need to decide what type of power packs you want. I chose handheld walkaround throttles with memory. These allow you to run a train, unplug the throttle from a socket, and move to a different socket while the train continues

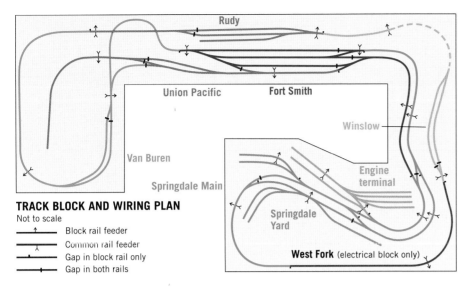

TRACK BLOCK AND WIRING PLAN

Not to scale

↑———— Block rail feeder
⅄———— Common rail feeder
⊢———— Gap in block rail only
⊢┼———— Gap in both rails

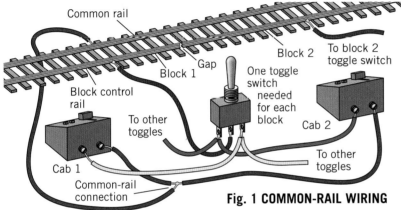

Fig. 1 COMMON-RAIL WIRING

Common rail
Gap
Block control rail
Block 1
Block 2
One toggle switch needed for each block
To block 2 toggle switch
To other toggles
To other toggles
Cab 1
Cab 2
Common-rail connection

Fig. 2 RAIL GAPS. Cut the rail gaps with a razor saw, then glue small pieces of .010″ styrene into the gaps to ensure that the rail ends stay apart. Trim the styrene to shape with a hobby knife and files.

at the same direction and speed. I bought two Chicago Model International (CMI) Blue Hoggers. These have base units that can be mounted under the layout, with handheld throttles that plug into standard telephone jacks.

I wanted to keep the number of electrical blocks to a minimum, but not have so few as to hinder operation. Considering the size of trains and the fact that I would be operating alone most of the time, I've found ten blocks to be just about right. That includes six on the main line and one each for the Union Pacific, Fort Smith Yard, Springdale Yard, and the engine terminal.

If you'll regularly have more than one operator, having more blocks will increase the layout's flexibility. See chapter 7 in *Easy Model Railroad Wiring.*

Since we used power-routing turnouts, which allow you to cut off power to spurs and sidings to store engines and trains, you really don't need a lot of extra electrical blocks.

Rail gaps

The track plan shows where I cut gaps in the rails with a razor saw. When using power-routing turnouts, you must feed electricity from the point ends and gap the rails between turnouts that meet frog to frog. You'll also have to add gaps to the block control (non-common) rail to mark the boundaries of each electrical block. See fig. 2.

Control panels

The control panels are simple and easy to understand. I also wanted them to be flush with the front of the layout. I decided to make Plexiglas sandwich panels, which

consist of a clear acrylic plastic (such as Plexiglas) front, paper with the schematic drawing in the middle, and the base. I simply used the fascia (¼″ Masonite hardboard) as the base.

My panels are local, meaning I have several small panels located around the layout near the areas they control. If you wish you could instead make a centralized panel, with all of the toggle switches located on one panel, with a track diagram of the entire layout. I find that the local panels are easy to follow as well as unobtrusive.

I drew the schematics on a computer and printed them using a color printer. You could just as easily use a ruler and colored markers (or colored pinstriping tape) to get similar results.

Place the acrylic over the printed schematic and use a marker to locate the holes for the toggle switches. Drill a small pilot hole for each switch, and also drill holes for the mounting screws. Use a ⁷⁄₃₂″ bit to drill the final holes for the switches.

Locate the acrylic on the fascia. Use a 1¼″ bit to drill clearance holes for the toggle switches in the fascia. Place the paper schematic and acrylic back on the fascia, lining up the toggle switch holes. Hold it in place, drill mounting holes, and add the mounting screws.

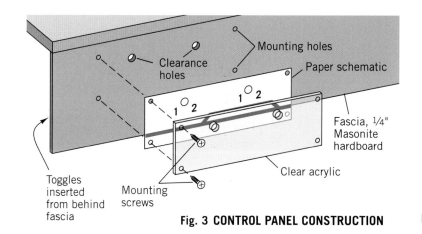

Fig. 3 **CONTROL PANEL CONSTRUCTION**

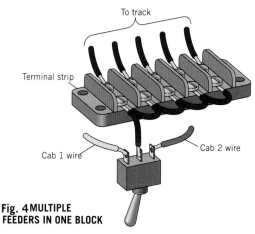

Fig. 4 **MULTIPLE FEEDERS IN ONE BLOCK**

Bill of materials

Radio Shack
279-450 dual modular wall plate (3)
275-651 SPST toggle switch (15)
275-654 SPDT center off toggle switch (10)
274-670 terminal strip (60

Chicago Model International
Hogger Blue walkaround power packs (20

Miscellaneous
16-gauge stranded wire:
    white (75 feet)
    brown (75 feet)
22-gauge solid-core wire:
    red (100 feet)
    black (100 feet)
24-gauge four-conductor telephone wire
    (75 feet)
clear acrylic sheet
solder, rosin core

Wiring the toggle switches

Color coding the wiring helps keep it organized. For example, my block control wire is black, the common rail is red, cab 1 is white, and cab 2 is brown.

Solder 12"-long wires to all toggle switches at the workbench. It's easier than doing it while crawling under the layout. Install the toggle switches from the back of the fascia through the holes on the control panels and tighten the toggle switch nuts.

Feeders and bus wires

I started wiring with the common rail feeders. The track plan shows the locations of all the feeder wires, with the arrow heads marking the block rail side and the arrow tails marking the common rail. To get through the foam base you can use a long drill bit, or you can use an awl or other sharp object to simply poke a hole. Make each hole as close to the rail as possible. The AMI Instant Roadbed will easily hide the hole once the wire is in place.

Solder a two-foot piece of red insulated 22-gauge solid wire to the rail. Then prepare the wire by stripping the insulation from about ½" of the end, and bend a right angle ⅛" from the end. Add the block control feeders in the same manner, but using black wire.

Next add the common rail bus (main) wire. This will help get some of those feeder wires out of your way. I used red 16-gauge stranded wire. It simply runs from the power packs around the back side of the layout (see fig. 1) and terminates at the end on a terminal strip. Strip back the insulation on the main wire and solder the red feeders in place. Keep feeders as short as possible.

The power pack wires take a little more time, but are still fairly simple. You need to run a wire from the remaining terminal of each power pack to one pole on each toggle switch. See fig. 1. Run two 16-gauge wires—white for cab 1, brown for cab 2—around the front of the layout. At each control panel, strip the insulation from the power pack wire and add the feeder or feeders from the toggle switches.

The center pin of each toggle switch must be soldered to its block control feeder. Some individual blocks had more than one feeder wire. For these, run the feeders into terminal strips, then simply hook the center wire to the correct terminal. See fig. 4.

Throttle wiring

The handheld throttles on CMI's Blue Hoggers use standard four-wire telephone cable and connectors. I added simple two-jack phone plates in three convenient locations along the fascia.

Wiring the jacks was easy. Run a standard telephone cable from cab 1 to the top jack of the first plate. Run another set of wires from this to the top jack of the second plate, then the third. Do the same for cab 2, but using the bottom jack on each plate.

That's it. You're wired!

Scenery for the A&M

Ballasting track, adding rock castings, and
planting foliage on our N scale project layout

By Mark Watson | Photos by the author

Welcome back to the N scale Arkansas & Missouri project layout.
Although trains have been plying the rails, something about the
track just doesn't look right. We'll fix that with paint and ballast, two
key elements toward making toy trains look realistic. We'll also add
portals to our tunnel and plant some trees and foliage to get rid of
the "golf course look."

Painting track

Painting track tones down the plastic appearance of the ties and kills the unrealistic shine of the rail sides. Using different colors can also help differentiate between the main line and sidings.

Start by placing small pieces of tape over the pivots and points of all the turnouts, as the paint can act as

Two RS-1s lead a freight into Winslow, Ark., on Mark Watson's N scale Arkansas & Missouri layout. Details such as rock outcroppings, foliage, and painted and weathered track help a layout come alive.

an electrical insulator and keep the turnouts from operating properly.

An airbrush and water-based paints are ideal for painting track. If you don't have an airbrush you can use spray cans (see fig. 1), but only if your layout room has adequate ventilation, and wear a respirator.

Work in small areas. This will give you time to clean off the tops of the rails with a Bright Boy before the paint completely sets. I used Polly Scale Grimy Black on the main line and Railroad Tie Brown and Rust for spurs and sidings. Spray the track from directly above as well as

Fig. 1 PAINTING TRACK. Clean the track with a Bright Boy abrasive block as soon as the paint dries.

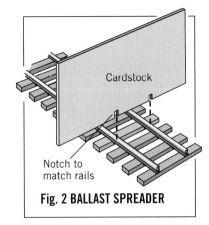

Cardstock

Notch to match rails

Fig. 2 BALLAST SPREADER

Fig. 3 GLUING BALLAST. Use an old glue bottle to thoroughly soak the ballast with the diluted white glue mix.

Fig. 4 WEATHERING TRACK. Use an airbrush to add grimy highlights along the track and ballast.

Fig. 5 TUNNEL PORTALS. The south portal (prototype and model shown above, top row) is concrete with stone block retaining walls, while the north portal (prototype and model bottom row) has a stone face with poured concrete retaining walls.

from either side to coat both the ties and rails.

Ballast

I settled on two different colors of Woodland Scenics fine ballast: buff for the A&M track and light gray for the Union Pacific track at Van Buren.

Place a small amount of ballast in a small disposable plastic cup. This is easy to handle and regulates the amount of ballast that you can dump. Gently shake the cup back and forth following the direction of the track. When the ballast covers the ties, you have enough.

The next step is to smooth out the ballast. I use a soft medium-sized brush and a piece of stiff cardstock with notches cut out for the rails. See fig. 2. Hold the cardstock at a 45-degree angle to the rails and gently pull it along to distribute the ballast. Use the brush to move any ballast that isn't cooperating with the cardstock.

When the contour of the ballast is just the way you want, spray it with "wet water." I start with one quart of water, five drops of dish detergent, and four tablespoons of denatured alcohol. The soap and alcohol will help the mix penetrate the ballast without disturbing it. Place this mixture in a pump spray bottle and soak the ballast. Don't spray too close to the track or you'll blow the ballast away before it has a chance to get wet.

Once the ballast is wet, mix a 1:1 solution of water and white glue with a couple drops of liquid dish detergent. Using an old glue bottle as a dispenser, set the cap to a steady drip and apply the mixture. See fig. 3. It's important to thoroughly saturate the area. If you use too little glue, only the top part of the ballast will be bonded, creating a thin crust that will eventually break away.

Be careful around turnouts. The glue mix will flow wherever the track is wet, so it's easy to glue the switch points and throw rod in place. To keep the points free, flip each turnout back and forth a few times as the glue dries.

After the ballast is dry, push a freight car with metal wheels around the layout to detect any ballast that may have found its way onto the rails. Use a hobby knife to remove the stray pieces.

Weathering track

It's easiest to use an airbrush to weather the track, because we're only looking for a light mist to tone down the ballast and further weather the rails. See fig. 4.

I use the same mixture of Polly Scale Grimy Black, thinned 1:1 with distilled water, for all the track. I applied it more heavily in some areas, such as on the tracks around the engine terminal and around turnouts.

Tunnel portals

Each tunnel portal on the prototype A&M has a different construction style. The north portal has a stone block face with smooth concrete retaining walls and is dark gray. The south portal has a concrete face with stone block retaining walls and is light gray. See fig. 5.

I used Chooch single-track concrete portals for both. To replicate the look of the north portal I simply used a scriber and straightedge to cut some blocks into the face. Both portals were a little short compared to the prototype, so I fixed this by placing a piece of ¼" foam core under each side. See fig. 6. Run this foam core back from the portals approximately 6", also using it to support the tunnel wall.

Casting the retaining walls was

Fig. 11 COLORING ROCKS. RIGHT: Create shadow details with a wash of India ink and alcohol.

Fig. 12 HIGHLIGHTS. FAR RIGHT: Drybrushing with white paint adds highlights to the rocks.

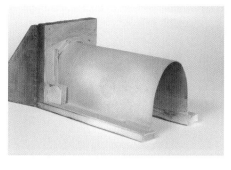

Fig. 6 TUNNEL WALL. Use foam core under each leg of the portal. The interior is .020" styrene.

Fig. 7 RETAINING WALLS. Use a foam core form to cast the walls in plaster.

Fig. 8 PLACING PORTALS. After gluing the portals in place, use wadded newspaper to create a basic form. Cover this with plaster gauze and a light coat of plaster or Sculptamold.

Fig. 9 PLACING ROCK CASTINGS. Play with the arrangement, then glue the castings in place.

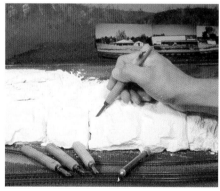

Fig. 10 CARVING ROCKS. A hobby knife and carving tools work well for blending castings.

Fig. 13 MAKING TREES. Add texture by spraying with hair spray and adding fine ground foam.

Fig. 14 PLANTING TREES. Poke a hole into the foam, add a drop of white glue, and add the tree.

fairly easy using ¼" foam core as fig. 7 shows. Cut patterns for both walls in one piece of foam core, then use paper clamps to secure this pattern to a foam core base. Pour in the plaster and tap the sides to help eliminate bubbles. When the plaster sets, remove the clamps and gently remove the castings from the mold.

Leave the north retaining walls smooth (but clean up the edges) and scribe blocks in the south walls.

Use Walthers Goo to attach the retaining walls to the portal faces. Add an interior wall made from .020" styrene as in fig. 6. Paint the south portal Polly Scale Concrete and the north one Reefer Gray.

Position the portals on the layout. Find the tallest and longest freight cars you plan to use and test-run them through the portals to make sure they clear. Use Goo to glue the portal assemblies to the layout. Figure 8 shows how to blend the portals into the surrounding scenery.

Rocks and more rocks

I used several rock molds from Woodland Scenics, but you can use any number of molds from many companies. You can also buy pre-cast plaster rocks from Woodland Scenics and others.

Casting rocks is easy. Start by placing the mold on a level surface (a small tray filled with sand works well for holding molds). Mix the plaster, then pour it into the mold. Tap the mold a few times to release any trapped air bubbles. When the plaster sets, gently peel the mold away from the casting.

As the photos show I placed rock outcroppings in many areas, such as around the tunnel portals and bridges, on the hill below Rudy, and on the hill behind the station at Springdale. Figure 9 shows how I located several castings around the south tunnel portal.

Play with the arrangements and try several different combinations before gluing the castings in place. Don't be afraid to break some of the castings apart. This can sometimes lead to great-looking and unique rocks. I tried to get the castings as close to each other as possible. Also, don't be afraid to carve away part of the existing foam scenery to plant a casting.

I like to use a hot glue gun to attach the rock molds to the scenery. The glue sets up in seconds, so you can immediately proceed to the next step.

Fill in the gaps between the castings with the same plaster used to make the castings. This ensures that paint washes will have a consistent look. Figure 10 shows how I carved the plaster to blend the rocks together and into the landscape.

Following a formula from Dave Frary's fine book *How to Build Realistic Model Railroad Scenery* (published by Kalmbach), I used a mixture of 1½ cups of a 3:1 water/latex paint mixture added to 2½ cups of water. (Be sure to use the same earth-color paint that you used for the base scenery.)

Put this mixture into a trigger spray bottle and spray the castings. Create shadow effects by using an eyedropper to apply a wash of India ink and alcohol to the various recesses and crevasses. See fig. 11.

Once that's dry, highlight the rocks by using a flat brush to dry-brush white onto the ridges. To do this, dip the brush in paint and then run it back and forth on a paper towel until most of the paint is gone. Then lightly stroke the brush across the surface of the rock casting. As fig. 12 shows, the raised areas of the castings will catch the remaining paint from the brush, creating highlights.

Texture, bushes, and trees

The even, green golf course look was an improvement over bare foam board, but it's time to take it a step further. Scenic texture is what really starts making a train board look like a layout.

For the moment we'll ignore the areas where the towns will be.

I used several different colors of coarse ground foam. On the level areas I simply added what ground foam I thought looked good and sprayed everything with wet water. Soaking the foam with the white glue mix ensured that the foam wasn't going anywhere.

It can be tricky getting coarse and extra coarse foam to stick to the many steep hillsides. One solution is to fill a bowl a quarter full with a mix of 3 parts white glue and 7 parts water. Add a bag of coarse ground foam to the bucket and let the foam soak up the glue mix. It will look like a mess, but trust me—the glue will dry clear. Put on a rubber glove, pull out a handful of

Bill of materials

Chooch
9577 single-track concrete tunnel portals (1 pack)

Floquil paint
130007 Rail Brown spray
130013 Grimy Black spray

Polly Scale paint
414113 Reefer White
414116 Reefer Gray
414137 Grimy Black
414317 Concrete
414323 Rust
414329 Railroad Tie Brown

Woodland Scenics
34 extra coarse turf, yellow grass
37 extra coarse turf, medium green (2)
38 extra coarse turf, dark green (2)
44 burnt grass turf
49 blended turf, green (6)
63 coarse turf, light green
64 coarse turf, medium green (2)
65 coarse turf, dark green
73 buff ballast (4)
74 light gray ballast (1)
1101 tree kits, assorted colors (15)
1203 plaster cloth (2)
1230 rock molds (1 package)

Miscellaneous
denatured alcohol
foam core, ¼" thick
plaster
white glue

The Fort Smith Turn rolls across one of the A&M's high steel bridges behind a trio of C-420s. Trees and foliage fill the valley, just as they do on the real thing.

Make the tree kits according to the instructions and place a bunch of them on a piece of scrap foam board. Spray the trees with a generous amount of cheap hair spray and sprinkle on fine ground foam. I used Woodland Scenics burnt grass turf. See fig. 13. Add a second (light) coat of hair spray and set the trees aside until you're ready to plant them.

To plant a tree, poke a hole into the foam base large enough for the tree trunk, dip the trunk into some white glue, and stick it in place. See fig. 14. Start by planting all of the trees that would be difficult to reach once all of the buildings are in place.

Bridging the gap

It's high time we added the Micro Engineering girders and towers. Build the towers and girders according to the instructions. Lightly sand the tops of the girder sections to remove the paint. Using cyanoacrylate adhesive (CA), glue the girders to the underside of the track. I held the girders in place using twist ties (as come with garbage bags) as shown in fig. 15.

The towers were next. Cut off any unnecessary material from the bottoms of the towers (it's okay if the legs hover a couple of scale feet off the ground). Use more twist ties to glue the towers to the girders.

The bridge abutments (fig. 15) are ¼" foam core with styrene edges and

are painted Polly Scale Concrete. Push the top of each abutment to the bottom of the girders and use hot glue to attach the abutment to the foam subroadbed.

Add bits and pieces of rock castings as well as coarse ground foam around the abutments to blend them into the landscape. At the feet of the towers, build up small mounds with ground foam and sand and fix them in place with the wetting solution and diluted white glue mixture.

Fig. 15 BRIDGE AND ABUTMENTS. Use twist ties to hold the girders in place, then the towers. The abutments are glued to the foam scenery base.

soaked ground foam, and place it on the surface. If the foam still wants to slide down, use push pins or map pins to hold the foam in place. Remove the pins when the glue dries.

Trees

I've built more than 400 trees so far, and I could still use many more. Most are Woodland Scenics kits, but I made a few using weeds as branches and course ground foam for foliage.

Structures for the A&M

Building towns at the workbench
for our N scale project layout

By Mark Watson | Photos by the author

It's time for the buildings to go up, so put on your hardhat and let's get started. I've found that it's not necessary to have dead-accurate models for every structure to capture the flavor of a town. Instead, scratchbuild or kitbash the most recognizable structures, then use the closest available kits for all of the other buildings.

I decided to model the small business districts of Rudy and Winslow as closely as possible. Springdale has a few scratchbuilt and kitbashed structures, but about half of the buildings are straight from kits. In Van Buren only the depot was kitbashed—the rest of the buildings are, for the most part, straight from the box with a few added details.

Area-specific signs make a world of difference in capturing an area. The addition of other more generic store, advertising, and detail signs also helps make scenes come to life.

Cities at a time

I did as much work as possible at the workbench, then transferred completed groups of buildings—and entire towns—to the layout.

Using Winslow as an example, start by cutting a paper template to the exact size and shape of the town base. Include roads, streets, and bases for structures on the piece.

Cut a piece of ¼"-thick foam core ½" smaller than the template for the sub-base. Then cut a piece of .040" styrene the exact size of the template, including roads. You can get styrene sheets up to 4 x 8 feet from plastics dealers in medium-size and larger cities—check the Yellow Pages.

Test-fit the foam core base and styrene at the layout. File the bottom edge of the ends of the roads at an angle. This allows the styrene to line up slightly below the railheads. Glue the styrene to the base using Walthers Goo.

Adding structures

As you complete each structure, glue it to the base in the correct

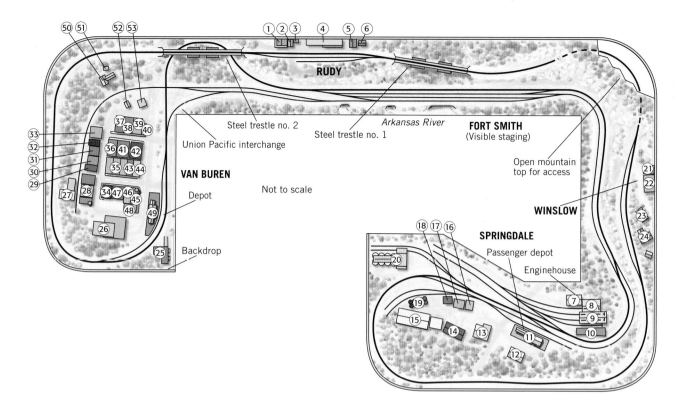

location. Weathering the roads (using various colors of powdered chalks applied with a brush) and adding people and vehicles really make the towns come alive.

Glue the town to the layout using latex Liquid Nails. I used nails along the edges to keep the base pressed firmly to the layout until the adhesive dried.

Use small pieces of rock castings, coarse ground foam, and dirt to blend in the edges of the town base with the surrounding scenery.

The structure key shows building locations on the track plan. Feel free to substitute other buildings or detail them to suit your taste.

Structure key

Key   Part number and manufacturer
Rudy

1	60-101 Arrowhead Scale Models convenience store (Hensley Grocery)
2	622 American Model Builders Dill's Market
3	18 Kestrel Designs yard hut
4	Scratchbuilt (Carney building)
5	Scratchbuilt (fire station)
6	3 Kestrel Designs bungalow

Springdale

7	55003 Micro Engineering Petroff Plumbing (A&M offices)
8, 9	60001 Micro Engineering modern enginehouses
10	Design Preservation Models wall sections (Ozark Valley Products)
11	627 American Model Builders UP depot
12	60011 Piko Warwick Workshops (Napco warehouse)
13	661 DPM Olsen Feeds (QVS Furniture)
14	55002 Micro Engineering Transworld truck terminal
15	55007 Micro Engineering Doyle Distributing (Southwest By-Products)
16	55002 Micro Engineering Transworld terminal (Butterfield Vet and Farm Supply)
17	933-3200 Walthers Interstate Fuel (Butterfield)
18	Scratchbuilt (Tyson)
19	933-3200 Walthers Interstate Fuel (Southwest By-Products)
20	933-3225 Walthers ADM grain elevator (Tyson)

Winslow

21	Scratchbuilt (South building)
22	Scratchbuilt (Mercantile/City Hall)
23	7464 Life-Like rural chapel
24	1513 Model Power farm house

Van Buren

25	661 DPM Larsen's Implement
26	660 DPM Woods Furniture
27	60010 Piko Warwick Guitar Factory
28	933-3224 Walthers Merchants Row II
29-31	501 DPM Bruce's Bakery
32	511 DPM Cricket's Saloon
33	508 DPM Crestone Credit Union
34	502 DPM Hayes Hardware
35	535 Period Miniatures Merchants Row
36	504 DPM Char's Soda Shop
37	508 DPM Crestone Credit Union
38	501 DPM Bruce's Bakery
39	933-3210 Walthers theater (King's Opera House)
40	507 DPM Corner Apothecary
41	514 DPM Erik's Emporium
42	504 DPM Char's Soda Shop
43	512 DPM Roadkill Cafe
44	507 DPM Corner Apothecary
45	513 DPM corner turret building (Rawford County Bank)
46	511 DPM Cricket's Saloon
47	504 DPM Char's Soda Shop
48	512 DPM Roadkill Cafe
49	683 Con-Cor smalltown station
50	45812 Bachmann farm house
51	605 AMB Sonny's Shack
52	65139 Micro Engineering 1940s gas station (closed gas station)
53	55003 Micro Engineering Petroff Plumbing (race car garage)